the PASTOR
and
MARRIAGE
GROUP
COUNSELING

the PASTOR
and
MARRIAGE
GROUP
COUNSELING

by

Richard B. Wilke

Nashville   ABINGDON ⓕ PRESS   New York

THE PASTOR AND MARRIAGE GROUP COUNSELING

Library of Congress Cataloging in Publication Data

WILKE, RICHARD B.   1930-
The pastor and marriage group counseling.
Bibliography: p. 1. Marriage counseling.
I. Title. 2. Group counseling. 3. Pastoral counseling.
HQ10.W487   253.5   73-18351

ISBN 0-687-30129-7

The poetry on p. 82 is from "The Cocktail Party" by T. S. Eliot.
Used by permission of the publishers, Harcourt Brace Jovanovich,
Inc.

Scripture quotations unless otherwise noted are from the Revised
Standard Version of the Bible, copyrighted 1946, 1952, and 1971
by the Division of Christian Education, National Council of
Churches, and are used by permission.

MANUFACTURED BY THE PARTHENON PRESS AT
NASHVILLE, TENNESSEE, UNITED STATES OF AMERICA

dedicated to the couples who trusted
a pastor and his wife
and
to our children—
Stephen, Paul, Susan, and Sarah—
who went to bed by themselves
and understood.

Foreword

Dr. Paul Popenoe, of the American Institute of Family Relations in Los Angeles and one of the early pioneers of marriage counseling in North America, once made a remark which I have never forgotten. "We shall not begin to meet the needs of this country for marriage counseling," he said, "until we train pastors on a large scale to do the job. Pastors are to be found in every community in the United States, large and small. They are in daily contact with the people, and the people trust them. They see the sad consequences of marriage failure as no other section of the community does. Instead of devoting our efforts to the training of professional specialists, we should give every pastor in the land a basic training in marriage counseling."

I have devoted most of my life, here and in other lands, to the training of marriage counselors. Many of them have become professional specialists, and I am proud of the work they are doing. But I acknowledge that this kind of highly specialized counseling service touches only a tiny fraction of the vast multitude of married couples who need help. I have therefore tended more and more to realize the soundness of Paul Popenoe's analysis.

When Richard Wilke's manuscript came into my hands, therefore, I read it with considerable enthusiasm; and I am delighted to have the opportunity in this Foreword to commend it to its readers. I hope these will include many clergymen; but I hope they will also include many other persons, both professional and lay, who are concerned about the disconcertingly high rate of marriage failure in our contemporary society.

I am well aware that in recent years a great many books have appeared about marriage and about marriage counseling. The question may well be asked—"Do we need yet another? Does this one say anything new?" My answer to that question is an emphatic yes. This book *is* different, and it says something new that is of considerable importance. Let me try to substantiate that statement.

The major problem of the clergyman today, as I see it, is that he has such a plethora of roles that he tends to be fragmented and consequently disoriented. He is expected to preach, to teach, to organize, to visit his people in their homes and in hospitals, to counsel them privately, to preside at baptisms, weddings, and funerals, to be involved in community affairs, and to be a diligent student of theology and of social life. This does not exhaust the list of his duties; but the attempt to perform these duties certainly exhausts *him!*

The effect of all these pressures is to make the clergyman not only weary but disillusioned. He has a growing sense of frustration because he seems to be touching human life and human beings more and more superficially. And in the process he has so little time left to devote to his own family that his relationship with his wife and children may also become superficial. I have for some years been increasingly concerned about what is happening to the marriages of clergymen. Again and again I have seen the wife of a pastor either lose all vital interest in her husband's world and cease to give him the support he needs or try desperately to find a way of sharing his life significantly, only to realize that she seems inextricably locked into a subservient role.

In this dilemma, gifted clergymen are giving up and seeking other vocations. Many of them are going into work which involves a good deal of counseling and are finding that they are at last grappling with real human situations in a way that brings them fulfillment. Yet all they are doing is to employ the gifts which led them into the ministry, and which by a grim, ironic twist of fate could only find expression outside the ministry. This seems to me to be not merely a disturbing but an intolerable situation.

I see Richard Wilke as a clergyman who has found one way of breaking through this impasse, and in his testimony I see great promise for many others.

First, he has chosen to concentrate his counseling ministry on married couples. That is a wise choice. With an obstinacy that borders on pathology, our culture seems unable to grasp the fact that marriage is the nuclear human relationship upon which all others ultimately depend. Study after study reveals that personality disorder and social maladjustment, in their myriad forms, result almost entirely, directly or indirectly, from family malfunctioning; and it is simple logic that family malfunctioning results almost entirely from *marital* malfunctioning. To put it the other way round, the child of a warm, loving, creative marriage is almost certain to become a responsible and creative member of human society. So if we want to redeem society, the obvious place to begin is with marriage, the place where love begins and life begins and the family begins.

Pastors are not unaware of this. They do of course get involved to a considerable extent in marriage counseling. But most of them lack either the training or the time to do it very effectively; and doing it ineffectively is highly discouraging to all concerned. So the clergyman's attempts to grapple with marriage problems all too often add to his general discouragement rather than relieve it.

Here is where this book offers the promise of something better. Richard Wilke encourages pastors to undertake what he calls "marriage group counseling." At first sight, this might seem threatening to the clergymen. There is a widespread idea that if counseling with one couple is difficult, counseling with five or six couples together is so complicated that it should not even be considered. So, few persons do consider it.

However, Pastor Wilke challenges this idea—and I am ready to support him. For eleven years my wife and I have been working with groups of married couples and studying the interactions among them. One of our most significant discoveries has been the manner in which the couples in the group, once they have established openness and trust, help and support and heal one another. We have felt so confident about this that we have experimented, entirely successfully, in the training of carefully selected lay couples to lead such groups. These lay couples have never yet fallen into serious trouble. When they have been perplexed about what to do next, they have called on the group itself to help them; and this has never failed to resolve the difficulty.

These groups of course have been designed for marriage enrichment rather than therapy. But the dividing line is often difficult to draw. Care in the selection of the couples should eliminate those with obvious pathology; and consultation with a skilled clinician will provide guidance in an emergency.

Of course the clergyman should seek whatever training he can get for this work. But it is necessary to point out that every clergyman already possesses basic competence in dealing with groups of people. To a far greater extent than most other professionals, he is engaged in dealing with human interaction during most of his time. No clergyman can get far if he is unobservant of people's reactions, insensitive to their feelings, or unable to tolerate their expressions of emotional stress. The average clergyman, therefore, already has a built-in competence in the art of leading and facilitating groups. Unless he has had special training for his counseling role, my guess is that he would do more good, and less harm, in counseling couples in groups than in counseling them individually. And in that way he could conserve his time so as not to neglect his other duties.

Above all, Richard Wilke stresses the essentially religious nature of the marriage group counseling he has pioneered. Unlike many pastors who take up counseling, he defines what he does squarely in terms of a religious ministry. In his groups people pray together. They seek forgiveness. They repent of their sins. They practice *koinonia*. No one can say this is going outside the province of the clergyman and invading the territory of the professional therapist. These activities are at the heart of ministry, and always have been. And it is in the small group banded together in Christian fellowship that these vital religious experiences always become dynamic and effective.

In short, here is a pastoral activity that will banish disillusionment. In leading married couples groups the pastor is supremely fulfilling his ministry. He is offering vital religion to the world in microcosm—for what is the world but a series of communities based on family units? He is putting religion to the vital test in a group of people who have struggled unsuccessfully to live together in love and peace.

All this Richard Wilke is very sure about. He writes

persuasively and with a contagious enthusiasm. He is telling us good news. This has worked for him, and he believes it can work for others. So he believes, and I believe it too.

I wish this book the success it deserves. If a mere fraction of the 235,000 parish clergymen in the land could follow the example of Richard Wilke, the gains to them, to their wives, to the churches, and to large numbers of American marriages would be incalculable.

David R. Mace

Bowman Gray Medical School, Winston-Salem, N.C.

Contents

Chapter I
Help! Help!

Virginia Woolf Lives Next Door

Hell has a new definition in America. Instead of fire and brimstone, it's tears and trouble at home. A quagmire of household anguish seeps across the sills in town and city. Some say there's an unhappy couple behind every other porchlight in the land. Twenty million people have been divorced since World War II. The family doctor, the president of the university, the state senator—even the minister in the neighboring town—all are having marriage problems. Our hardheaded editor recently mused in the local paper:

> If your neighborhood is like most, the morning coffee conversation is about the latest batch of divorces. There are sweet young things who were married too soon. And there are the sour middling couples that seemingly have been married too long. There are re-matches of re-matches. And it is all sad—a soap opera right in the next block.[1]

The local pastor feels the "vibes." He's poignantly aware of this nightmare of estrangement. He's experientially involved. Right now ministers, priests, and rabbis are doing

80 percent of the counseling in our country. Most of it has to do with family problems. The typical parish telephone rings steadily with trouble calls. I've jotted down some pleas for help which I've received—along with my inner reactions.

Pastor, you've got to help us. My husband and I have been fighting all night. He says he's going to leave, and I don't know what to do. Please come over and talk to him before he goes.

(Even if I go over, will it help? They've been fighting off and on for years. It will take a miracle to change anything. What will I say?)

My husband has threatened to commit suicide, and I am scared to death. I thought we had a really good marriage. I don't know what's the matter.

(Good grief. Am I a psychiatrist? What if I get involved and he does shoot himself? Maybe I should make a referral.)

I know that he is sleeping with another woman. Every time I get in bed with him, it's like there were three of us between the sheets. I am about to go out of my mind. Twice I've threatened to file for divorce, but I'm no spring chicken; maybe I couldn't find another husband. How could he do this to me and the kids?

(Dear Jesus, what a mess people make of their lives. I doubt if he will even talk to me. If I go to him, he'll be defensive as the devil. If I tell him to stop seeing that gal he'll tell me to go to hell.)

He drinks 'til two in the morning and comes home like a slobbering bum. I've had it up to here. If he doesn't shape up, the kids and I are moving out, and he can sleep with his bottle. Damned if I care.

(I wonder how much he drinks. Maybe she's exaggerating. Or maybe he really is an alcoholic like she says. She obviously still loves him or why would she show so

much emotion? Yet she seems tough as nails. How in
thunder can the church help?)

My mother-in-law said you might be able to help us.
My wife filed for divorce three weeks ago, and we're not
living together, but we're both miserable. She'll come with
me, if you can see us.
(Boy, it's the eleventh hour. They've been married
nine years, have had three kids and buried one. They
both have "stepped out" a few times, and they have
bills all over town.)

An Autobiography of Frustration

How does a minister or priest respond to family problems? I've tried almost everything. Like most local pastors,
I've scratched out methods of ministry the way a barnyard
rooster searches for food. It's been hunt and peck. I've
groped, studied, and counseled in an effort to help couples
who were in trouble. Sometimes the act of priestly listening
to a confession helped restore a marriage relationship. Occasionally, a referral to a competent counselor helped a
home, but these experiences were spotty. Usually the problem is not one of confession but one of communication.
Often a good referral is hard to find. Besides, when people
need neither medical nor psychiatric care, a pastor would
like to be of help—in the name of God and the church.

In seminary I had been schooled in Rogerian nondirec-
tive counseling, now called "client-centered therapy." That
was good. Most ministers talk too much and listen too
little. (One psychiatrist said that it took him several years
to say "Ummm" so that it meant "I'm listening—I'm not
judging you—please go on.") I learned to "empathize" and
listen reflectively. But not enough happened, particularly
with marriage problems. Couples would talk to me for a
time or two, say that things were better, and go their way.

19

Sometimes I had helped them over a rough spot. More often, I had taken away a God-given stress which might have forced a life-changing reappraisal. I felt as if I were putting band-aids on abscesses.

I began to structure appointments over a period of weeks. With encouragement from Dr. Don Groskreutz, Lutheran professor and psychologist, I suggested long-term procedures. I proposed to couples that it might take weeks, even months, to unravel the mess they were in. I began individually with two or three couples. That's not many each week, but those interviews expended what little extra time and energy I had. Some healing took place. We drained off a lot of bubbling hostility. Husbands and wives began looking at each other again. Communications were reestablished in areas from sex to finance. Still, just when we needed to plow deeper, to realign habit patterns, to experience a new form of love, progress halted. My methodology and skill ran thin. When counseling was terminated, the couple often had no involvement in the church, no fellowship with other couples, and no plan for future growth.

Something else happened that shook my structures. A gynecologist became interested in my work. Dr. Norman Harris began referring anxious, troubled women with severe marital difficulties. Before long I was trying to see couples during supper hours, late at night, and on Saturdays and Sundays. My family began to complain, and my parish work started to suffer. I desperately needed to consolidate. If only there were some way to work effectively with all of them at one time. It seemed as if Providence were pushing me to find a better method. For the first time I began to think seriously about group work.

I wondered what to call this "group-child" about to be born. The term "spiritual therapy" suggested that it was going to duck the gutty issues of money and sex and somebody slugging somebody else with a frying pan. "Prayer therapy" sounded to some like a Wednesday night prayer meeting. "Treatment group" was more appropriate to a clinical setting.

The most likely term for a church ministry seemed to be "marriage group counseling" or "marriage therapy group." Therapy, in the broad sense simply means healing, and the church has had a healing ministry for twenty centuries. The word "marriage" helps to distinguish the method from psychoanalytic group therapy. As I prepared for the first group, I explained that we would be involved in therapy for sick marriages.

However, "therapy" is often thought of as a medical term. Professional therapists rightly cherish special credentials. Some couples were a bit frightened by such an awesome term. Later on, I began to feel more comfortable with the expression "marriage group counseling." It sidesteps the medical image, picks up on a growing acceptance of pastoral counseling, and avoids using a technical term. It builds on the marriage counseling already being done on an individual basis.[2]

Looking for Resources

Little has been written for pastors on group counseling or group therapy—practically nothing about *marriage* groups. However like most ministers and priests, I had seen the power of therapeutic fellowship, notably in Alcoholics Anonymous. Also, I had participated in prayer-sharing groups where there existed a sense of openness and sharing. Numerous books stressed the healing power of *koinonia* fellowship. Though precious little material was directly aimed at distressed marriages, group life seemed to hold promise.

Two resources came to my attention. A friend of mine, the Reverend Harold Nelson, had been working with a small group of people in his church using the Yokefellow plan of psychological testing and sharing. The process is described in *Prayer Can Change Your Life*.[3] The authors, William R. Parker and Elaine St. Johns, discuss in detail a prayer-therapy group which had been conducted under carefully controlled conditions. The group was continually involved in psychological testing, guided by the group therapist. They were committed to daily prayer for one another, quiet personal meditation, and genuine openness within the group. The Yokefellow program provides a testing service beginning with the Minnesota Multiphasic Personality Inventory Test. It then furnishes "insight slips" every two weeks for twenty-two weeks which are shared and discussed within the group. Although the group described in *Prayer Can Change Your Life* was made up of troubled individuals, not couples, it was apparent to me that the same process would work effectively if both husbands and wives were present.

The second resource was introduced to me by an Episcopalian priest. A Catholic marriage counselor, Urban Steinmetz of Escanaba, Michigan, had put together a series of talks called "A Marriage Enrichment Seminar." Under a foundation known as the Family Enrichment Bureau, these records were made available to pastors, priests, and concerned laymen, not for therapy but for enrichment of marriage relations. Leaders were encouraged to get a half dozen couples together, listen to the records, and then spend some time in serious discussion of them. Steinmetz had a disarming way of presenting material—unassuming and very low-key—combined with a frankness and openness, which was refreshing even on records. It was appropriate material to include as a part of our group counseling strategy. Subjects covered included "communications in the home," "understanding ourselves," "achieving sexual enjoyment," "acceptance," "dollars and sense," and "raising emotionally healthy children." The dynamics of group process had to be well established before these records were used; but in that context, couples quickly moved into significant interaction.

The Struggle to Begin Group Work

Armed with these resources, and frankly desperate for a new strategy, I set a date and struggled to get a group together. It is difficult to form a group, not because there are too few troubled couples, but because there are so many fears involved, so many resistances to overcome. For a man or woman to ask for help requires an act of humility, a "lowering of the plumes." Quarreling couples are especially fearful. Then when a counselor suggests a group setting, which implies airing problems with other people, the anxiety level really shoots up. A pastor has to be as reassuring and forceful when he suggests group participation as a doctor proposing surgery.

I began with two couples who were already working with me in a conjoint counseling procedure. One of these couples belonged to the congregation. The other marriage was one I had performed a year previous—a divorcee with four teen-aged sons and a thirty-eight-year-old bachelor. Several professional people in my congregation encouraged me to attempt the group work. They promised to refer troubled couples to me. Soon my telephone was ringing.

Dr. Harris referred several couples. Because his contact was usually with the women, I had to struggle to get the men involved. His medical referral provided helpful leverage. Referrals from the attorneys did not have the medical or psychiatric evaluation behind them, but usually they tended to include both man and woman. Couples coming by referral were more serious about commitment to counseling than "drop-in" members of the congregation or those who had simply called the nearest church. Often with referrals I was able to have two or three individual or conjoint sessions, indicate that I was ready to start group work, and contract with them to enter the group.

As the time for organizing the group drew near, I did not hesitate to encourage, even plead with other possible participants. Here is the time to be aggressive. For example, Evelyn, an inactive member of the church, first started calling me with regard to her fifteen-year-old daughter. The girl was unusually mature physically but typically immature emotionally. According to her mother, the girl's jeans were getting tighter, her grades poorer, her hours at the skating rink longer. But the more Evelyn and I visited, the more evident it was that there was a breakdown in their marriage. Her husband Harry had a mania for work. Sometimes he would work all night. When he was home, he was indifferent to Evelyn's pent-up feelings, indulgent toward the children, and "once removed" from the emotional life of the family. Evelyn, unsupported in disciplinary matters, overdid it with a kind of nagging, nervous intensity that seemed to alienate her daughter and send her husband back to work. So I went to see Harry at his office and said something like this: "I'm not here to meddle, but as you know, Evelyn has been in to see me a number of times. Your daughter is rebellious and probably headed for trouble, and your wife is about to climb the wall. She sometimes mentions divorce. I'm here to run up a red flag and to say that your home is in serious trouble." He replied that he knew things were bad but he didn't realize how bad. Tears came to his eyes. I told him I would be glad to recommend a clinical psychologist or, since our group was just getting started, he and his wife could come to it. They came the following Wednesday night and never missed a meeting. Once Harry drove two hundred miles in order to be present.

What Happened?

At our first meeting we had six couples. My wife was a kind of participant-helper. We met in the living room of our parsonage because there was no informal room in the church, and we wanted a warm, homey atmosphere. We met for eight months, meeting for two hours each Wednesday night. The following year we had five couples and the third year we had seven couples. Each group met weekly for seven to nine months. During the fourth year I did not conduct a group myself, but helped another pastor form a group.

In each of my groups, we concluded with a fairly extensive written evaluation by each individual. (The evaluation form is given in Appendix A.) Not only did they evaluate the group experience for themselves, but they were asked to analyze what had happened to their mates. They also were asked to ascertain changes in other couples in the group. About half of the couples claimed for themselves dramatic changes in communication, self-understanding, and release from hostility and guilt. These observations were verified by others in the group. An additional

25

one-fourth of the couples received significant help, enough so that they answered the question "Would you rather be where you were before the group began or where you are now?" with an emphatic "now." They indicated areas (sexual, financial, etc.) where they still needed a lot of improvement, but they seemed to have the problems more clearly in focus and in a more manageable form. Within each of my three groups there were inevitably one or two couples who received little help. In my first group, we had one couple leave the second week because I was "pushy" in a sensitive area. I asked Bess, a frightened and insecure woman, a pointed question which dealt with sexual relationships. She poured out some highly emotional and personal material; but then she became embarrassed. She and her husband did not come to another meeting of the group in spite of my encouragement. I counted them as a casualty of my inexperience. Now I understand "kairos"—letting the bud of the flower open without forcing it.

Other failures (or very low success level couples) will be discussed elsewhere, but they include a highly structured authoritative man who tended to dominate the group. After a short time, he began working nights and dropped out. He and his wife were later divorced. Two other couples showed little progress: they were highly dpendent upon one another and very hostile because of that dependency. Our evaluation would show about twenty-five percent who were not helped significantly. Most of these, however, expressed appreciation for the experience, for the friendships that had been formed, and for the opportunity to share some of their feelings.

Recently I compared our results with those reported by two psychologists who are in private practice. They prepared a questionnaire, similar to ours, except that it included multiple choice questions as well as essay questions. It was a bit more sophisticated and used independent judges to evaluate the questionnaires. The leaders, Jeanette Targow and Robert Zwerber, were cotherapists, male and female, and had conducted four separate, open-ended groups. The maximum size was four couples, mostly in the thirty to forty age range, predominantly college graduates and upper-middle income range. The length of treatment varied from one month to two and one-half years. Husbands and wives generally agreed on the value of help received. The judges evaluated that two-thirds of the couples experienced moderate to great change in relationship and one-third of the couples, little or no change.

> As a whole, the essay responses stressed improved communication; this was mentioned directly in seventeen responses. Reduction of fights and irritable exchanges between partners, improved sexual relationships, and improved relationships with the children were cited by a large number of respondents.[4]

Frankly, I was happy with the comparison between our results and those of Targow and Zwerber. We did not work for as long a time, our groups were larger, and we included a higher percentage of people from lower educational and economic classes. Our level of improvement was slightly higher. The Targow and Zwerber study stressed improved communications. So did ours. But in addition we received numerous comments that described a deeper experience of faith and love. Here is a sampling of our subjective evaluations. A fifty-year-old woman, with an eighth grade education, had a number of physical symptoms and had been referred by Dr. Harris:

When I began to unload my fears, my burdens became lighter. My headaches began to taper off. I didn't have to have as much medicine. [This observation was authenticated by Dr. Harris.] My days became happier. I had longer periods between deep depression when I didn't bottle my feelings up so tight. I began to let go and do a little fighting for my own beliefs. I had lots of problems which I refused to face. I began to see other people had problems as great as mine. I still didn't tell all that is bothering me (some of this material came out later in psychiatric and pastoral interviews). A very deep love grew for each other in the class. There have been several times this past year I have really visited with God and what a marvelous experience it is to know he still cares for me.

A thirty-five-year-old salesman, a high school graduate, who worked on the road all week wrote:

I have come to understand myself better and accept my shortcomings more readily. I have been able to communicate more freely with and feel more at ease with my wife. I believe she has gained a better understanding of me and my feelings and the things in life that are important to me.

Under five categories of change he wrote:

a) financial—the best in twelve years b) relationship to children—perhaps more patience and understanding c) sexual—no change, d) family—inlaws—still satisfactory, e) communications—much better on both parts. (This couple, with several children, began climbing out of nearly $15,000 worth of personal debt.)

His wife was so frightened that she often sat up all night whenever he was gone. She sat in a chair, watching both front and back doors with a shotgun on her lap. She wrote:

Our marriage was in terrible shape—in fact barely even existing at all. . . . As time progressed people began to trust the others in the group and would open up with many problems and feelings that they would hesitate to discuss with anyone else or any other group. My husband is able to better understand my feelings and ideas. I have been able to more accept myself as I am. Also the short-comings within myself. I have been able to rid myself of guilt, self-consciousness, self-pity. Not completely—but at least in part.

Harry, the man I called on to "raise a red flag," wrote:

Words cannot explain the effect the group has had upon my relationship with God. What does it say in the Bible? Do not come to worship me and ask forgiveness until you have forgiven your brother. In the group you truly under-stand the full meaning of this. . . . a) financial—The debts are still there but are not the mental worry they were before. I have come to understand that the best things in life are truly free and that my financial problems are just another man-made mistake, and with God's help I will carry them, live with them, and dispose of them as God allows. b) relationship with children—(Remember his fifteen-year-old rebellious daughter?) Never in the short span of our children have our relationships been so rewarding. Now I can truly say that my children come before my work. c) sexual—great, man, great. After find-ing the true meaning of sexual desires and the commitment of the act and the climax, I understand the beauty in man's sexual relationship with his wife as God intends.

There has been a slow gradual change of oral com-munications and a change in the nonverbal communica-tion. The time we spend together is not nearly as bad as it was but not nearly as good as it should be. One of the greatest changes in my wife was not using liquor as a night cap and sleeping pill. I could see that she had used the liquor as a crutch because she did not have me to lean on.

29

Harry's story is important enough to dwell upon at length. At the conclusion of our eight months of group counseling, Harry and Evelyn attended a Family Spiritual Life Camp, where Harry had an experience with God which has now, in the span of three years, influenced his family, his church, and to some extent the entire community. Here is his testimony:

> At camp we were asked to find a psalm from which we gathered strength. I didn't even know which part of the Bible the psalms were in. That afternoon and evening I tried to find a psalm that would lift me up, but I could only get from them what my life had been—lustful, dishonest, self-pleasure seeking, sinful. The next morning when it came my turn to tell what psalm meant so much to me, I fell completely to pieces and broke down and cried like a baby. All of the emotions I had built up for years came out. This was the first time I could remember of ever letting down my guard and releasing all the pressure that had built up within me. Then the most wonderful thing happened. The leader asked the rest of the group to pray for me. This was the most wonderful experience I had ever had in my life. That same afternoon I went to the top of a knoll outside our cabin and asked God to forgive me and take hold of my life for it now belonged to him. This is when I realized that I had been reborn.

It would be important to add perhaps that Harry, a highly educated professional man, has become a leader in the church and a strong advocate of missionary, evangelistic, and social work. Like a number of others, he still has to work hard at communication within his family, particularly with regard to his willingness to share his feelings, but he is doing it. He and a number of others have helped form dialogical or sharing groups within the church which help maintain their openness and concern for others.

The Reverend and Mrs. Marshall Stanton organized their first group and worked intensively for five months. I asked him to write an evaluation. His experiences paralleled my own.

When I had counseled with some of my parishioners for a couple of years and was not making significant progress, I knew that something more must be done. In some instances professional counseling by a psychiatrist had already been tried without noticeable help. I knew that I had taken them about as far as I could. My own personality became a barrier at times. At other times I could see that even though I understood their problems, I was not capable of communicating with them. Even when we could share on an intellectual basis, there was no progress emotionally. I discovered that diagnosis was not enough; there had to be therapy which I did not know how to give.

When I learned of a plan of psychological testing and group therapy, it seemed to offer a new dimension of help. After investigating its potential and talking with Richard Wilke who has used the resources in different groups, I became convinced that it was worth trying.

Some of the values of the marriage counseling group are outlined here:
1. The entire approach gave a new kind of structure in which to work.
   a. The group committed itself to a task for a long period of time (five months initially with an option for longer).
   b. Expectations were that all would share the responsibility for helping each other.
   c. I would not be the final authority but the convener and moderator.
   d. By using reliable psychological testing procedures, insights into ourselves would be gained.
   e. My wife and I were both participants in the group, having taken the tests and having shared as did any other participants.

31

      f. Sharing of the psychological insights became the basic material of our sessions.

2. Each person becomes a counselor. As the group process developed and as people began to respond, the value of the group approach became obvious. Those people with whom I had counseled were helped by others who could identify emotionally with them. People began to talk, support, and question each other in a way I, as one person, could not.

3. After two months of meeting once a week for two hours, some small changes began to occur.

      a. One saccharine-sweet woman discovered that behind her always smiling face was enough hostility and guilt to start a war. When she was able to confess that, accept it as a part of her, realize that hate and love coexist in her, and face it all, she began to feel freer than she had for years.

      b. Henry's stresses with his wife were many. He, the successful businessman, had so repressed emotions all his life that he could not feel. This especially was true of his feelings towards his wife. He was handling his emotions by burying them. The small but significant change for him has come in seeing that others have handled their emotions in a similar manner but have successfully learned to acknowledge them.

      c. Mary came with a frightened withdrawn look about her. As she was given, not forced, an opportunity to share, she slowly ventured out of her shell. Her very appearance has changed. She doesn't sit and look at the floor now. As the group has accepted her, she looks more relaxed. Her difficulties are far from over; her feelings of inferiority are still great; but she has changed.

4. Values for the ministry of the church: The group process produces a dynamic unavailable to me personally as a counselor. I believe that I have discovered a key to an important phase of my over-all ministry in the group process with which I did not have experience

previously. It is an exciting thing to watch people get some help when I know how deep their stresses and pains are.

Professional Evaluations

All forms of spiritual, emotional, or marital growth are difficult to measure. Clergymen tend to look at church participation for signs. About one-half of the couples saw a connection between their church life and the healing work of God in the group. Those who were already a part of the church seemed to be stronger in their commitment. After we terminated one counseling group, it became a study sharing group without my involvement. Attorneys tended to evaluate in terms of divorce proceedings which were dropped and trouble calls that terminated. (Parenthetically, some attorneys are changing their policy on fees. Instead of charging a package fee for an entire divorce proceeding, they are simply charging for their time in consultation, making a charge if a divorce is filed, with additional charges if it is concluded. In this way, they do not have as great a financial interest in seeing the divorce finalized. That is a more professional approach.)

Dr. Harris observed the following signs of growth when he evaluated his patients: (a) a decrease or cessation of medication (pain medication, tranquilizers, sleeping tablets); (b) less criticism of mate and a more positive outlook toward life; (c) insight into the true nature of their problems; (d) a creative attempt to cope with those problems.

Sex, for some couples, became beautiful for the first time. Especially in cases where a tense, high-strung, frustrated, guilt-ridden woman was married to a quiet, hard-working undemonstrative husband, a new sexual orientation developed. Although little was shared openly in the group, comments in doctors' offices and pastors' studies indicated the change. Men came to understand the needs of their wives for reassurance, for deep level communication, for time spent in whispering, love making, fondling. Women began to see their role in sex play as a more active, creative one. Several couples showed by visible appearance a new found emotional and physical well-being.

It is always a thrill for a pastor to see people becoming increasingly receptive to spiritual experiences and service opportunities outside counseling. The work of the Holy Spirit is not limited to the group sessions. One woman was released from resentment and found freedom to forgive in a religious retreat. Children of couples became active in our youth groups. One car salesman began a plan of daily prayer and meditation on his own initiative. He has continued it for several years. Another man, whose father was an alcoholic, agreed to serve on the board of directors of a halfway house for alcoholics. Jim and Mary, who lost their baby in childbirth, have encouraged and counseled other people in grief. Sometimes they lend a helpful book, write an encouraging note, or give prayer support. Although smoking was never mentioned (we placed ash trays in our livingroom), two men decided to quit smoking. One couple began singing in the choir. Two couples are teaching church school classes. George, in another town, although still not active in his church, became a supportive friend to his pastor. Sam, who when he was ten years old thought he was not good enough to belong to the YMCA, was baptized and now serves as an usher of the church.

An Evaluation of Myself

It became apparent to me, that we had touched on some realities of life. My ministry suddenly became alive again.

Wednesday night became the most exciting night of the week. Although I hesitated for months before I had the courage to begin the group work, once it started it provided me more joy than any other phase of my ministry. Instead of working hand to mouth, haphazard, piecemeal, I now had a plan. Healing things were happening. I had rediscovered a clue to the meaning of the church.

The pastoral task involves the curing of souls and the realigning of marital relationships. The pastor, with normal training and experience, has assets and opportunities which would make many psychologists and psychiatrists envious. I am convinced that God intends for the church to be an agent for healing. The Church is the "body of Jesus." It ought to be performing his ministry in the world. My present dedication, and the purpose of writing this book is to try to persuade churchmen that marriage group counseling is a practical, person-centered method of ministry. It can restore family relationships and open doors for encounter with God.

Chapter II
From the Individual
to the Group

From the world of psychoanalytic practice and also from the experiences of contemporary Christian life, one idea seems to be emerging. People can be healed in group encounter. This idea has been slow in coming and even now meets with suspicion, both by some psychoanalysts and by some churchmen. Pastors and counselors have hesitated to structure group counseling, particularly for married couples. Yet this approach is so valuable that it will not be denied. The emergence of group treatment is so dynamic that it is rattling the structures of pastoral and secular counseling.

Historical Roots of Group Therapy

The whole rise of contemporary group therapy would be a fascinating study, but it can only be sketched here. Joseph H. Pratt, a Boston physician, is credited for being the first person to make use of a group method for scientific treatment purposes. In 1905, Pratt gathered tubercular slum patients together to explain hygiene, diet, and medications.

He also provided inspiration to sustain patients' morale. Pratt's colleagues were skeptical of his endeavors, but he was given both encouragement and financial support from the Emmanuel Episcopal Church and its minister, the Reverend Elwood Worchester. Another physician who pioneered group methods was a minister who became a psychiatrist, L. Cody Marsh (1928). The church, which ought to know the potential for healing in corporate life but has often forgotten it, has nevertheless played and continues to play a role in the discovery and scientific application of the group method.

The work of Kurt Lewin spawned all kinds of studies and experimentation in the social sciences, educational circles, and religious groups. His diagrams of field theory and his experimental study of human relations made people aware of the dynamics within group life. Group process was distinguished from group action. What was going on emotionally in a group was delineated from the "minutes of the meeting." An infinite variety of groups today reflect Lewin's pioneering efforts. The plethora of group life evidences the hunger for interpersonal relations which our society is experiencing. Human relations laboratories, sensitivity training groups, prayer fellowships, and hosts of other approaches with countless varieties now have appeared on the scene, many of which are helpful and meaningful for specific purposes. Aberrations are to be expected. Some will remember in the 1950s when some young seminarian or "expert" in religious education had read part of a book on group dynamics and delighted in creating anxiety at a lab school or workshop by structuring a leaderless group or an agendaless agenda. Worse, in the 1960s some psychologists and "human relations" leaders attempted highly emotional sensitivity experiences with inadequate training and structure, sometimes doing considerable harm.

Clinical work has been going on in group form all over the country. Much of it has been hesitant and gradual. Many doctors and therapists have been feeling their way. Usually they have been working with a group of individuals rather than with a group of couples.

Roadblocks to Group Work

Freud and His Couch

There have been many obstacles to overcome. Freudian analysis emphasized the relationship between the doctor and the patient. So did Rogerian client-centered counseling. The one-to-one, therapist-client involvement took on an aura of sanctity. But today, there is an increased awareness that there is also a social dimension to healing which can not be overlooked. Isolation and physical separation, relics of nineteenth-century psychiatry, are being abandoned in favor of community life within many mental hospitals. Today mental health centers are built right in the city or town instead of "off somewhere." Usually there is a closer family involvement in the total therapy program than was the case a few years ago. Dr. Neal Daniels of the Philadelphia General Hospital writes:

> There are many forces at work today breaking down the traditional isolation of the mental health facility from the larger community. Changes are taking place in the definition of patient status, with a growing consideration for the imbalances in patient-family relationships. Programs are being devised to modify the artificial separation of the patient from his original family setting. By including the state hospital in the orbit of the local community and by providing psychiatric facilities in general hospitals, the sheer fact of physical separation is being

overcome. Bringing the mental health facility back into the community increases the opportunities for contact with the family of the patient and tends to raise even more urgently the role of the family in the care of the hospitalized patient.[1]

Some of us recall recent experiences when doctors would not even talk to members of the family of an emotionally ill patient. Patients were often isolated for long periods of time from pastors and friends. This quarantine existed in spite of men like Federn, who went so far in 1943 as to predict cure only if the family wished it. Some doctors now advocate the acceptance of the entire nuclear family, rather than the individual patient, as the functional unit in psychiatry.

In most progressive hospitals and clinics today, there is a continuing effort to maintain relationships with the family insofar as possible. At one of the best private hospitals in the country, Prairie View Hospital in Newton, Kansas, members of the family are in regular consultation with doctors and counselors. Pastors are encouraged to visit their sick parishioners. Patients are permitted to go home for weekends as soon as they are able. There is a general openness to human encounter. I recently referred a seriously disturbed woman to Prairie View. A part of her treatment was in group therapy. Her husband sat with the doctor on a regular weekly basis. He visited his wife every few days. The chaplain wrote me a letter encouraging me to make regular visits. The woman was in church with her family on weekends while she was still hospitalized. When she returned home after six weeks, it was not difficult for her to make the transition.

Professor Hulme is not thinking of psychoanalysis but rather of counseling when he proclaims rather dramatically:

> We are breaking with Freud and his couch. Our concern now is for group progress and social structure. . . . This trend has shifted the focus from the therapeutic *relationship* to the therapeutic *community*. . . . Freud's biological concepts have been corrected by social understanding. A person does not become a human being except in the context of community.[2]

That is overstatement, but it is a helpful corrective to the one-to-one doctrine in which many counselors, especially pastors, have been steeped.

Preoccupation With the Past

In addition to the emphasis on family context, attention is being paid to the present instead of the past. Springing from various schools of thought, with sundry slogans such as "reality therapy," "logotherapy," "existential psychology," transactional analysis," "gestalt counseling," etc., most counselors are abandoning the desire to rummage about in past experiences. Counselors are focusing on the here and now feelings instead of the then and there. Therapists emphasize present decisions. This trend is especially true in the field of marital conflict.

Counselors and pastors used to spend much time trying to figure out why people feel the way they do. We analyzed early childhood experiences to learn how people were molded into their present behaviour patterns. We found, however, that just learning why did not necessarily bring about change. There was a fog of determinism in the air. I remember a number of years ago taking a course in personality theory. Near the end of the course, the professor,

who was not a counselor at all, and who knew more about
rats in mazes than he did about people, asked, "Do you
think that our growing knowledge of human behavior will,
one of these days, enable us to accurately predict individual
and group behavior?" I was dumbfounded; over fifty stu-
dents nodded affirmatively. Slowly I raised my hand and
said, "I don't think that the human personality can be
completely measured by the scientific method. In spite of
great influences, I think that there is a spark of freedom
within a human being which makes absolute determinism
impossible and behavior, therefore, not completely predict-
able." There was a moment of dead silence. Then, from the
back of the room, a man called out, "That sounds like a
religious idea to me." I was delighted. What he meant to
be derision, I knew to be the truth.

That truth is being recognized throughout the psychological world today—if not as a religious idea, at least as
a corrective concept to an overemphasis on determined
behavior. I was recently involved in a two day seminar with
six couples, working with a chaplain who is trained in
transactional analysis. In the midst of the group, he worked
directly with individuals. Often a dialogue developed between the leader and one participant. The interchange
would go something like this:

Mother: "I'm a compulsive housekeeper because my
mother kept nagging at me all the time when
I was a girl. Nothing was ever clean enough for
her. Now I can never sit down—I'm always
rearranging or dusting or scrubbing—and I'm
yelling at my kids the same way my mother
did."

Leader: "Do you like to be this way?"

Mother: "No. No. I'm not happy. And I'm going to

41

	make my kids the way I am, and they won't be happy either."
Leader:	"Why don't you change?"
Mother:	"I can't."
Leader:	"Humm. Would you consider saying 'I won't' or 'I don't want to change?' "
Mother:	(shaking her head negatively) "No, that isn't what I want to say."
Leader:	"What do you want to say?"
Mother:	"I want to say that I want to be different."
Leader:	"In what specific way?"
Mother:	"I want to be able to sit down in the evening and visit with my children, even—even if there is a coat on the chair or a glass on the kitchen counter."
Leader:	"Why don't you decide to do that?" (Long silence as the entire group sat quietly. Big tears welled up in the young woman's eyes. Finally, she said words that seemed almost magical.)
Mother:	"I've decided. I am still going to keep the house clean, but now when I see a book on the table or a glass in the sink, I'm going to say to myself that other things are more important to me and my family."
Leader:	"What would your mother think?"
Mother:	(The woman's reply was full of insight and maturity.) "You know, Mother's house wasn't always perfect, even though she yelled a lot. Besides, it's my life to live. I'm of age; I can keep my house the way I want to."

To be sure, this experience took place within a group filled with acceptance and love support. Admittedly there was some time for peering into childhood reasons for our feelings. Yet the fantastic emphasis on *present* handling of feelings and the *decisional* redirecting of behavior is a dramatic contrast to orientations dealing primarily with the past. Maybe it's like Abraham Lincoln said: "Most people are about as happy as they make up their minds to be."

Empathy

Another change in strategy is a shift from empathy to challenge. Or, we might think of this pendulum swing as movement from the subjective to the objective, from an emphasis on the expression of feelings to a recognition of the responsibility for behavior. In the theological world it would be analogous to speak of moving from an imminent to a transcendent view of God. Somehow the counselor and the therapeutic situation stands "over and against" the client. The counselor has overt expectations. Accountability and responsibility are words that are OK to use once again.

Erich Fromm distinguishes between the symbolism of motherly love, which is an accepting love that sustains us through thick and thin, and fatherly love, which is a self respecting kind of love that we achieve. Both of course are essential. Every person needs an unconditional kind of acceptance—hopefully to be experienced as a tiny baby, but needed all our lives. But, as a balance, each person needs to feel worthwhile because of his actions and achievements. It's almost the same balance as many of St. Paul's letters: the first part tells of God's complete mercy in Jesus Christ; the second part places serious moral demands upon us as the people of God. Paul's understanding of grace can never be understood without his powerful "therefores." Or, to use another biblical analogy, the people who were miraculously saved by God, who was with them day and night, were also the people who received the moral demands on the stone tablets.

The truth is that we can be broken either way. We can be broken by overwhelming moral demands. Paul and

Wesley and Freud and Luther were overfathered. But we can also be destroyed by a smothering, pampering, continual babying which demands nothing. There are no heroes to point to here—such victims are squatting on a blanket somewhere waiting for mother to bring them another glass of warm milk.

Do you recall that incident in World War II when General Patton slapped the soldier who was shell-shocked and crying? It is fairly certain now that Patton did not fly off the handle. Instead he hoped to shock the man into self-respect. Patton had remembered a soldier in World War I who, he thought, was so supported in his self-pity that he never recovered. Patton decided to use a direct approach. I have never found out what happened to the soldier Patton slapped. I would like to know if that "father's slap" worked.

I remember hearing the psychologist William Glasser tell about his work with girls in reform school. After they had told him their plans to get even, to harm and hurt others and themselves, Glasser would ask this powerful "over and against" question: *"How will that help you?"* That question is a nice blend of support ("I'm interested in your welfare") and challenge ("I want you to strive for your own well-being").

I'm afraid that ministers of the gospel need this corrective as much for themselves as they do in their counseling. The pastorate has become too motherly. It's time for a little more "thus saith the Lord." The priestly role is supportive and important, but the prophetic task is demanding and essential, too. Many a pastor has had his self-respect eroded away by limiting his ministry to a "hand-holding" operation. Even if a congregation seems to desire a motherly pastor and even if such men often appear to be successful, it is more of a symptom of the sickness of the church than it is a sign of strength. I discovered that even the aggressive action of organizing marital counseling groups did something for my self-image. I found that I was seeing myself more as an effective agent for healing than I was a chaplain with a crying towel.

Changes in the Life of a Psychoanalyst

We have been discussing three correctives: movement from the individual to the family, from the past to the present, and from the subjective to the objective. As is often the case, this movement can be seen in the life of an individual therapist. A clear illustration is the work and writings of George R. Bach. His early training was in psychoanalysis, and he did considerable work with individual patients. He also studied the field theory of group dynamics under Kurt Lewin. Soon he was doing depth psychoanalytic procedures in group experiences, and in 1954 he wrote his classic *Intensive Group Psychotherapy,* which is a brilliant blend of those two approaches. Even though the book is group-oriented, it nevertheless uses analytic theory as its rationale for therapy. For example, there is material on wish drawings, dream interpretations, etc., and considerable effort is made to explore the feelings of the patients. Persons were chosen for the group on an individual basis. There was no attempt to work with married couples.

However, in 1968 Dr. Bach collaborated with Mr. Peter Wyden, a professional writer, to produce the best seller *The Intimate Enemy.* This popular book describes Dr. Bach's highly structured group technique that teaches couples "how to fight fair in love and marriage." Talk about objective! There are all sorts of rules to prohibit a man or woman from hitting below the belt. Furthermore, not much time is spent in going into the past. The key question is "How are you two people going to act and react with each other today and tomorrow?" His sessions spend very little time in analysis of the past; they are basically concerned with helping people formulate patterns of responsible behavior toward one another. Earlier, Bach was primarily concerned with individuals in groups; now he is working with married couples in groups. Earlier he stressed past feelings; now he is emphasizing immediate patterns of action. More than ever an advocate of group work, he writes:

> The training of groups, rather than individuals or couples, has considerable advantages. Group work is less expensive, faster and more effective. Couples quickly become less dependent on the therapist. The group mileau stimulates growth in a natural way. Trainees live out, for everyone to see, the patterns and postures that would only be talked about in individual sessions. And as group members question each other about their problems, they don't only weigh the then-and-there of what happened in the past; instead they demonstrate to everybody in the room the here-and-now of how they feel and what they're really all about. Candid challenges thrive in this atmosphere. Faking, blamesmanship, and digging into ancient psychiatric museums are reduced to a minimum.[3]

Marriage Counseling Groups

Joseph W. Knowles, minister and counselor-chaplain, has probably done more than any other person to lead ministers into concepts of group treatment. His book *Group Counseling* is included in the "Successful Pastoral Counseling" series.[4] He argues effectively that therapy groups are valuable tools for pastors within the life of the church. He commends group counseling to pastors as a "medicine

of choice" and insists that it has unique therapeutic resources which are not available in individual counseling.

But Knowles concerns himself only with troubled individuals and not with troubled marriages. His approach is to
work with disturbed individuals in a group setting, much
like Dr. Bach described in his early writings. Knowles even
argues against couples being in the same group. He says
that couples are more defensive in each other's presence.
Neither wishes to admit weakness or failure in the marriage
for fear that admissions may be used as ammunition by the
partner in subsequent battles. But our experience was quite
the contrary. In the first place, couples are much less defensive than in conjoint counseling. (The counselor often
ends up trying to be a referee.) But also the fact that each
couple around the circle is having problems—others seemingly more serious than one's own—relaxes the defenses.
As admissions of failure come forth, husbands and wives
have enough trust in the humanness of the group to reveal
themselves.

Knowles argues that hostility ventilated in the group will
supercharge negative feelings when they go home. In separate groups they ventilate feelings and arrive home with
a sense of release and clarification. But that is a distorted
conception of counseling. Many marriages don't know how
to communicate anger. Some husbands or wives have never
openly expressed hostility to their mates. But when they
see hostility ventilated within the rational atmosphere of
the group, they are not as frightened by it as they were.
They are like children putting a toe in the water—they find
that an honest "owning" of feelings isn't so bad after all.
Some evenings in a group, it seemed as if anger were a
living entity, flopping on the floor like a fish. We were able
to look at it and talk about it. When Knowles suggests get-

47

ting rid of pressure in the absence of the spouse, he side-steps the need to communicate anger to one another. If a couple learns how to fight fairly in the group, then they can learn how to fight fairly at home.

Knowles also thinks that groups will polarize on the basis of sex—men against the women. Again, we found exactly the opposite to be the case. People were concerned to see that everyone was treated fairly, regardless of sex. The women were toughest on the women, and the men were most severe on the men. To be sure, a discussion on "how a woman feels" or "how a man feels" might polarize the discussion for a time, but the discussion was usually quite helpful. The seating around the circle was significant. We were never a "Mennonite meeting" with the men on one side and the women on the other. People always sat where they wanted; inevitably the men and women were always mixed up.

I suspect that Knowles developed his arguments from theories rather than from experiences. They were certainly popular notions in psychoanalytic circles a few years ago. (Freud in 1908 said that if both marital partners needed help, they should not even go to the same therapist!) Or perhaps he had attempted at some time or other to introduce a couple into an otherwise individual-oriented group. That would not work. But if we are trying to bring healing to people in the context of marital distress, both husband and wife must be involved. My guess is that Knowles, like Bach and others, in more recent years has found this observation to be true.

Today, without any question, all sorts and types of marriage therapy groups are in existence throughout the country. Family service centers and professional counselors are rapidly moving into this form of therapy in much the same way that physicians began to use penicillin or the sulfas. Pastors are now beginning to feel more confident, due in part to an increased amount of clinical training. It is about time because there is so much work to be done. Here and there, pastors and chaplains are beginning to discover marriage group work as an authentic form of ministry.

One of the most interesting examples is the work of Chaplain C. L. Bruninga of the state hospital in Norwich, Connecticut. Several years ago the staff of the hospital realized that many of their discharged patients were coming back as patients again. In fact, the readmission rate was a discouraging 35 percent. These patients had been dismissed, had spent various lengths of time in the community, and then returned ill again. The observation was that although there were many reasons, the prime problem was a failure of marital readjustment. Therefore the staff asked Chaplain Bruninga to form a marital group counseling procedure.

A patient was required to have his spouse join him in the enterprise, patients could not attend without their partners. Some of the couples began the marriage group as their hospitalization neared completion; others waited until they had been dismissed. The group is called technically an "open group," i.e., it goes on all the time with couples on a waiting list to enter when another couple decides to leave.

The main interest of the group is problem solving. They decide that, no matter what the difficulty, there are only three possible solutions: accept the situation, change it, or separate yourself from it. In other words, divorce or separation was always a live option (as it really is, anyway). Yet the results were quite dramatic. After working with forty-eight couples, only two, according to Chaplain Bruninga, have separated, and one of these reunited. Even more im-

49

portant, only two of the forty-eight patients have returned to the hospital!

Since we are dealing with a minister of the gospel who is neither psychiatrist nor psychologist (though he has had clinical training) it is worthwhile to take a deep look at his evaluations. He writes:

> Why has the group been helpful? 1) The sense of isolation is reduced; they see others in similar conflicts. 2) New group members, hearing successful solutions by others, find their frustration and hopelessness abated. 3) Attempts to "stack the deck" against one's spouse are usually defeated by other members of the group. 4) Sensitive areas such as sexual problems are more easily discussed in a group than in individual sessions. 5) Solutions to problems usually represent the consensus of the group. The solutions have been tested by some and so are not easily ignored. [Note: Chaplain Bruninga is more problem solving in his orientation than most group leaders, certainly more so than my groups have been, but notice how that emphasizes present forms of behavior and responsible action.] 6) Helping other couples results in a sense of accomplishment and pride. It gives added incentive to tackle one's own problems. 7) The spirit of mutual concern comes close to duplicating a family circle.[5]

Keep in mind that these rather dramatic results were achieved with couples, at least one of whom had been institutionalized with mental illness. One conclusion of the staff deserves to be emphasized. *The psychiatric observing team believed that the therapeutic spirit within the marriage therapy group was enhanced because a chaplain led the group.* Apparently a clergyman can be incorporated into the "family circle" more easily than a physician or a social worker.

Many pastors have walked the trail described by one psychiatrist. First he did individual counseling. Then he did conjoint therapy. He later began working with another therapist, forming a small group of four. He read books, experimented, and finally launched into couples' groups. He found the group method often produced superior results. Pastors with experience in individual and couple counseling and with experience in small group process may well stand on the threshold of group counseling.

Actually it should be natural. The idea that healing occurs in community is as essential to our theology as faith itself. The church's historic witness is that redemption and healing occur as persons are reunited in fellowship with God and with his people. Group counseling may be a new approach to ministry for the pastor, but there is nothing new about the idea that he is meant to lead a therapeutic community, to guide a healing fellowship.

The well-known words of Earl D. Marsh are true: "By the crowd they have been broken; by the crowd they shall be healed." For our purposes it might be more appropriate to say, "By the family they have been broken; by the family they will be healed." It may well be that the current psychological and theological stress upon community will enable the church to recapture its powers of healing broken relationships. Certainly the future indicates that the rapid rise of various forms of group healing, including marriage group counseling, will be an effective style of Christian ministry.

Someone has said that "conventional religion has the words but not the music." Therapy groups can help people sing again. Again we have been criticized, as were the disciples of Kant, that "their hands are clean, but they have no hands!"

The needs of the world are the agenda for the church.

God will judge our present moment by how well we meet human need.

Phillip A. Anderson of the Chicago Theological Seminary writes:

> The members and ministers of churches have yet to fulfill the role which is rightfully theirs in helping troubled people. Our power over unclean spirits and our skill in healing every disease and infirmity are often unavailable or impotent (cf. Matt. 10:1). For too long the Christian fellowship has ignored or referred or kept carefully hidden the troubles of people. Yet the church in all generations, beginning with that of the New Testament, records experiences of healing and reconciliation. Such experiences of healing must be available within the Christian fellowship if we are to fulfil our role as disciples of Christ.[6]

The emerging form of group counseling for married couples can prove to be a needed instrument for well-trained pastors who are serious about helping troubled people. It will provide a "medicine of choice" in coping with a society of sick marriages.

Chapter III
Group Structure

What is the structure of a counseling group? What are its boundaries? How large is it? How long does it meet? What form does leadership take? These questions, and others, are important. Fortunately, there are answers born out of the experiences of many people.

Size

Joseph Havens, though not a counselor or therapist, has had a world of experience with group life. He writes, "By small groups I refer to units of six to fifteen people who meet regularly . . . to share deeply with one another what is going on in their lives." [1] The treatment-growth goal intensifies the process, so the group must necessarily be smaller. The maximum size for random individuals is about ten; for couples' groups it would be slightly larger—about five or six couples plus the counselor. A minimum number seems necessary, too. Five or six people are needed to provide proper process; a counselor with less than three couples would not be able to work effectively. Three to six couples seem to be the boundaries, with five couples plus the counselor or team of counselors the ideal.

Time Per Session

There are some "one shot" experiences which may be helpful where competent people like Bach have twenty-four to thirty-six hour marathons. However, my own strong bias and the weight of experience in the field is for weekly sessions lasting one and a half to two hours. Prairie View Hospital in Kansas and Chaplain Bruninga in Connecticut have sessions of one and a half hours. It seems to be well recognized that the "counseling hour" (usually fifty minutes) is inadequate for a group process. Some therapists are experimenting with four-hour sessions. In my own experience, with the hard work that goes on in group process, that length of time would be too exhausting. Consistently I have had a two-hour involvement, making it slightly more informal than a clinical setting (a cup of coffee, a little informal chit chat) but maintaining a fairly close discipline of two hours a session. Incidently, having mentioned Bach's marathons, let me hasten to add that he is now helping groups organize on a weekly basis for follow up work. Obviously, if we are trying to restructure a relationship which has been deteriorating for years, we could expect the couples to need regular, consistent, long-term involvement.

Duration

There are both open and closed groups. The open groups are essentially continual in their operation. From time to time a couple will leave the group and a new one will enter. Chaplain Bruninga's method follows this form:

couples may stay as long as they feel they are being helped and may terminate, in consultation with the group, whenever they wish. The two main advantages are, first, that there is a continuous, ongoing program available; that is, you don't have to round up a group to get started. Second, some people obviously need more help than others, and it is arbitrary to set the healing process by a predetermined time schedule. The disadvantages, however, are several. Although an open group might work in a large hospital where a waiting list could be maintained, it would be difficult for a pastor or counselor to maintain the volume necessary in order to have a non-ending group. More important, it takes considerable time and effort to develop the trust level within a group. A newcomer causes anxiety. Understanding the ground rules, getting the feel of the process, and becoming familiar with others in the group takes time. The group has to stop and deal with newcomers. In my experience the level of trust and caring which continually deepened was an essential factor in the healing process.

Closed groups, with a beginning and an ending, generally last between three to nine months. The Prairie View program is three months, although a couple can enroll in an additional series if they wish. A number of counselors work from three to six months with a group. My own groups met from October to May because that was the time I had available.

The great problem with closed groups is what to do with couples who need help when there is no group currently being organized or when the group has been formed and solidified. (In the first two or three sessions it is still possible to introduce a new couple.) There seem to be two answers. One, it is possible to work with a couple individually for a time, even "carry" them until the group is formed. Two, there is usually a need for several persons or agencies to be doing this kind of work, so that they can space formation of groups intermittently.

In urban settings, pastors and priests of different denominations can agree that some of their number are especially skilled in counseling and should be used as referral persons. A schedule of group formations can be developed so that every few months a new group will be formed. What an opportunity for ecumenical cooperation! In a rural or sparsely populated area, one church could be a referral center for all of the churches in the area. A group could be formed each year. In some cities, close cooperation with a Family Service Center could develop so that groups could be formed alternatingly. Spillover by the agency or the church would warrant help from the other. Because the average pastor never has quite enough counseling at any one time to make group counseling possible, it makes considerable sense to load one pastor up for a while. Later on another counselor can tackle the job by forming a new group with the help of his fellows. No doctor can practice alone; no pastoral counselor need do so either.

Place

Almost nothing has been written about the setting for marriage groups, the implication being that it makes little difference. Most clinics of Family Guidance Centers use a conference room or some other room large enough for the group. These rooms are generally characterized by their lack of character; they are sterile and impersonal. One reason we held our group sessions in our living room was the desire for informality and warmth. What better place to deal with family problems than in the home? People sat on the floor, took their shoes off in front of the fireplace, heard the children make their way to bed, and sipped on a cup of coffee. Sessions were no social hour; it was like home, or rather, maybe like home ought to be.

The Commonality of Pain

Without any question, one of the greatest forces for healing in any group is the awareness of each person that "we're all in the same boat." Across the years I've visited innumerable AA meetings, and I've noticed the release of anxiety for troubled persons just in knowing that others are having problems, too. In fact, it often seems that others have even worse problems. There is a common bond in this awareness of mutual distress whether we are talking about TOPS (Take Off Pounds Sensibly) or Smokers Anonymous or some psychotherapy group composed of teen-age boys. It is a frightening experience to feel all alone, to believe that you have the greatest problem in the world. I have had couples say that they thought everybody else had good, happy marriages. Many express the belief that although others might have problems, nobody else could possibly have as severe a problem as theirs. The one basic criterion for a marriage counseling or therapy group must be the inclusion only of couples who are in serious trouble.

That is why we must distinguish between counseling groups and other forms of small group life. For example, when I first began, I announced from the pulpit that I was beginning a "marriage enrichment group" on such and such a date. I did that to take the sharp edge off the counseling procedure. But that blurred the important distinction. Fortunately, the one couple who came as a result of this announcement had needs deep enough to be a part of the group. Now, although we have periodic enrichment experiences in our church, we carefully distinguish between them and counseling groups.

We are not talking about sensitivity training either, as educational or helpful as that might be under other circumstances. Sensitivity training was born after World War II as persons sought to find new ways of communications and to rediscover levels of feelings. The experience varies with the composition of the group, and more especially with the trainer. Sometimes the training consists of a live-in laboratory for ten or twelve days. Another structure is a weekend away. usually followed by about nine weekly meetings in the home town. "The participant may expect to discuss (a) how his own feelings, motivations, and strategies are experienced by himself and responded to by others; (b) how groups function, with particular effects of the individual on the group and of the group on the individual; and (c) the application of this knowledge to his life in general." [2] The majority of training participants do not experience sufficient suffering to seek professional counseling. For people who are seriously disturbed or highly anxious, sensitivity training can be disruptive and dangerous. "The framework of sensitivity training does not, nor is it intended to, provide for the degree of attention, the continuity of therapeutic contact, or the availability of medical aids essential in working with very sick persons. The most obvious difference between therapy groups and training groups is that the training group is for educational purposes and the therapy group is for therapeutic purposes." [3]

Each couple must come to the group out of a sense of pain. I recall a group that was skeptical of a particular couple who sat quietly for the first few weeks. The group was secretly suspicious that the couple was devoid of problems. That illusion was quickly dispelled the night it came out that they had been married four times, twice to each other, and that one of their daughters was currently in the state hospital. With those credentials, they were accepted as part of a family of needy people.

Who Should Be in the Group?

Skilled therapists, particularly those in the field of psychoanalysis, often try to balance their therapy groups with a careful selection of participants. Generally in marriage group counseling such balancing decisions are not necessary. For one thing, since both husband and wife are represented, there is an equal male-female ratio, plenty of dominant-passive relationships, and an assortment of personality types. The age range tends to be between twenty-five and fifty. Most of the couples have been married from ten to twenty years. A leader might exclude a couple because of age. For example, I would not place two seventeen-year-olds in a group composed of thirty- to forty-year-old couples. On the other hand, some mixture of ages is interesting and helpful. Our most recent group contained two couples who were in their early twenties. They had been married only two years. The rest of the group were in their thirties. The whole group tended to be a little younger than usual. Based on our work with five different groups, over 80 percent of our couples were in their thirties and early forties. They had been married long enough to have considerable "investment" in each other, and yet were so miserable that they did not want the future to be a mere extension of the past.

I have always hoped for the opportunity to work with a group of very young couples where the age would be restricted to about twenty-two years old as a maximum. I think the commonality of situation, the brittleness of the relationships, and that combination of youthful pride coupled with inexperience would be exciting and challenging for a counselor. Unfortunately, although the need is tremendous (one-half of all divorces in Kansas fall in this category), there is generally a hesitancy to seek help, a strong feeling that they just made a mistake in choosing a partner, and the conviction that freedom from the relationship will solve the problem.

Here is another important criterion for choosing people: is the problem *primarily* marital? Our couples thought of themselves as relatively normal people with marriages that were on the rocks. Although all sorts of personal problems were involved, the accent of the trouble was in terms of marital relationship. There is, of course, a fine line between personal and marital problems. Each continually affects the other. Yet there is a difference in counseling procedure. Intake interviews must evaluate and ascertain this difference. Dr. Linden and associates has indicated that "the goal of group marriage counseling is improvement in interpersonal relationships, particularly within marriage, rather than profound character change." [4]

Qualifications of that statement flood in upon me, however. Individuals make up marriages. I have observed persons work through repressed grief, free themselves from psychosomatic symptoms, and grow in personal accountability. Sometimes I think our groups were simply broadly defined therapy groups composed of couples. Yet the group had a common denominator—the people came in order to build a better marriage. A man might need to express some of his suicidal fears in order to come out of his shell and communicate again with his wife. But his principal goal was to share once again his deepest feelings with his mate. By focusing on dysfunctional marriages, we were free to work with individual hang-ups. We worked to heal old hurts and to initiate new relational processes so that homes might be happier and healthier. People quickly learned that if their marriages were to be different, they themselves had to change their attitudes and behavior patterns. We were not as problem-solving oriented as Bruninga nor as conflict-focused as Bach nor as narrowly marital as many Family Guidance Groups. Within the broad range of marital distress, we worked on problems as they surfaced.

Unsuitable Persons

Nevertheless, having made this qualification, we still did not want people in the group who were too sick for us to help. The rule of thumb for the pastor is: does the person need psychiatric help? A depth study by several therapists on this subject indicates persons who are not suitable candidates.[5] Those with insufficient contact with reality are automatically excluded unless counseling is done in a hospital setting. Those whose behavior deviates from the group norm require a group of their own and the services of a specialist. For example, a marriage counseling group could deal with adultery and even with latent homosexual fears, but it would have insurmountable difficulties with a confirmed homosexual. Sociopathic personalities are to be screened out. They would delight in shocking the group with stories of deviant behavior. Knowles lists those with suicidal, homicidal, and infanticidal impulses as not suitable, but this should not be interpreted so stringently as to rule out people who have shouted, "I'm so mad I could kill

61

him" or those who at one point or another have thought about taking their lives. A doctor sent a man to us who had entertained self-destructive notions. Because of those negative feelings, he had asked his wife to lock up his hunting gun. The group was "just the ticket" for him. He was able to talk about some of his feelings without fear. On the other hand, the person clearly threatening to take his life should not be included.

People who are in catastrophic stress situations require individual counseling or referral. All sorts of examples come to mind. Here, for example, is a woman who has become pregnant while her husband was overseas. Now he is coming home. She panics. Or here is a couple whose little child has just drowned accidently in the bathtub. They are overwhelmed by guilt and grief. Later on, with some perspective, when the situation is no longer of emergency proportions, a group might be extremely effective. A group can be marvelously helpful for people who are working through residual grief or unresolved guilt. But extreme stress requires personal care. (Parenthetically, it might be noted that sometimes situations occur to couples who are in the process of group work. Sickness, loss of jobs, teenagers in trouble—life goes on. The group will pick up some of this, but during a severe stress, a couple may require personal consultation.)

Depression is always a matter of degree, but there are those who are acutely depressed and whose depression does not lift after consultation. Some can no longer function. A good rule for the pastor is to exclude those whom he feels he could not help in individual consultation.

Sometimes psychiatric care must precede marriage group counseling. On occasion, one member of the couple has been hospitalized. Then after receiving help, the couple was willing to focus on marriage difficulties. Sometimes they were exceptionally open and receptive.

Another kind of person who should not be included is the incessant talker. This person uses excessive talk as a defensive mechanism against disclosure of problems. A glaring failure in our five different groups involved a man who was overwhelmingly vocal, authoritative, and intellectual during the two months he participated. At that point his job schedule changed (deliberately?), and he dropped out of the group. He constantly challenged my leadership, created hostility within the group, and with his monopolistic tendencies, used up a lot of valuable time. If I had been more competent, I would either have excluded him originally or else I would have challenged his defense openly, quickly, and consistently in the group setting.

To summarize these unsuitable candidates, a graphic word from George Bach is well worth quoting.

> Many colleagues believe the success or failure of group therapy depends upon the effective selection and careful screening of individual candidates for group therapy. Faith in the value of screening and selection is often expressed by the idea that group therapy is like a caravan —it travels at the speed of the slowest member. There is indeed a caravan-like interdependency among members in therapy groups. But the analogy may be misleading unless one can say that the slowest camel tries to stay with the group and not get isolated in the desert. Naturally before the caravan starts it is wise to make a minimal selection and leave out those who are too sick, too young, or too burdened to walk and carry their share.[6]

People Likely to Be Helped

Some people are especially appropriate candidates. Those who are shy and who have not developed social skills will gain help because there is less pressure to talk than in individual counseling. Even people who are practically silent can be excellent participants. I recall one woman who was separated from her husband (he was working in another state, and they were contemplating divorce). By special agreement with the group and because she was under great stress, we included her in the group. Renée did not speak more than twenty sentences during the several months she participated, but after she rejoined her husband and they were reconciled, she wrote the following letter of appreciation to the group:

Being the last one to join this prayer therapy group, I imagine it was not easy for you to have me come. Nevertheless, you all accepted me so readily and with such a friendly feeling.

This all happened at a time when I needed help badly, and I found this help and understanding here in this group. Soon I realized this Wednesday evening meeting was very important to me, and I looked forward to coming each week. Being one of the less-spoken ones, I probably haven't contributed much, but your love and concern for me has done more good than you can imagine.

We know from the Bible that where two or three are gathered together in His name, He is in the midst. It's been especially meaningful for me to remember each of you personally in prayer, and this has been a part of my daily life. It seems when problems arise, I can turn to God in prayer once again, remembering each of you personally, and the problems grow small or disappear. This tells me that in helping and praying for others, we usually unknowingly help ourselves, too.

As a result of all this, I feel there are many things in many areas of life I can cope with now and many things I understand better. I will continue to remember each of you in my thoughts and prayers and hope the good that has come from this will be a continuing and growing experience for us all.

The most dramatic example of nonverbal participation is that of Leonard, age twenty-two. He and Kay had been married only a few months when he was given a military assignment in Europe. While there he developed an abssessed tooth, and the infection localized in his brain. Two or three operations were performed, and then he was discharged with 100 percent disability. Leonard, when I met him, was able to walk with a light limp, use only his left hand, read silently second grade material, write his name, and on occasion slowly say a single word. He left his wife, and she was heartbroken. Her Catholic faith and her real love for him caused her to want desperately to save the marriage. They had exhausted all medical help. He was not so deeply depressed as to warrant military hospitalization and psychiatric care. He was already involved in speech and physical therapy. I permitted Leonard and Kay to enter our group only because there was no place else for them to go. It was a young group, and Leonard's emotional responses seemed appropriate. During the total treatment experience, he spoke a maximum of a dozen words, but his nods, his nonverbal communications, his participation in the prayer circle were valid and helpful. One night he and Kay were absent, and the entire group felt their absence. In one of our concluding sessions, we went around the circle telling of any recent victories, joys, or satisfactions. Leonard was the last in the circle. But he completely "cracked up" the meeting when he forced out—one word— "pregnant." His wife nodded and beamed affirmation. The entire group vibrated with warmth and pleasure. Raymond J. Corsini calls this "spectator therapy." Often a person may just sit and observe, yet be deeply involved. Members will permit a person to participate in this way and will be quick to pick up his nonverbal communications.

Dependent people make good prospects for group life because dependency needs will be met by several in the group rather than totally by the counselor. Every pastor is familiar with such dependent people who take so much time. They often feel guilty themselves for being trapped in a helpless dependency on him. In contrast to individual counseling, group process lessens transference reactions toward the counselor. In a real sense, there are as many counselors as there are members. Members share responsibility, and come to depend upon each other for help.

> The dependency relationship is transferred from the pastor to the group. This is the same dynamic at work as that which operates in adolescence. Dependency is shifted from parents to the peer group, and a move toward autonomy is strengthened—precursor of a move toward inter-dependence in group relationships.[7]

Persons unaware of emotions and those who tend to repress anger are excellent choices. Every counselor is familiar with the person, often the male, who fights by withdrawal. He is what Bach calls the "dove." He is vicious. Many marriages are in difficulty because emotions are hidden and feelings unshared. A careful reading of the process notes for the Rutherford family (appendix B) will show a man who has been carefully trained across the years to hide his feelings.

Some individuals with psychosomatic symptoms do well in a group. Doctors have authenticated the physical improvement of such anxiety-produced symptoms as headaches, nervousness, ulcers, sleeplessness, impotency, obesity, and overdependence on medications.

Here are some red-hot prospects: a couple who can't

"hear" each other; a man and woman who have few mutual interests; and a husband and wife who can't clearly define each other's "role."

Round 'em Up

Where did we ever get the idea a pastor ought always to be passive? There are times when the shepherd ought to be actively searching for lost sheep. That's biblical, isn't it? He ought to be as aggressive as a cowboy lassoing a stray calf. If a couple needs group counseling, the pastor ought to make no bones about it. I've said all sorts of wild and ridiculous things, but I've generally made my point.

"Mary, it's taken twenty years for you to get in this mess. You shouldn't expect to get out of it without months of hard work. I wish I had a magic button, but I don't have one. But I can help you over the months ahead if you'll work with me."

Once I said, "Jack, you and your wife are going to hell on a bobsled. It's going to take all the power of God and man to save your home."

I've often used medical analogies with those who hesitated because of the expenditure of time and effort. "If you had cancer of the colon, you wouldn't hesitate to go to the Mayo Clinic, lose two months of work, and spend $5,000 to save your life. Well, your marriage has cancer. Aren't you willing to expend some time and energy to try to save it?"

Another kind of aggressive action open to the pastor is to go see people. A minister or priest can recruit like no other professional person. Recently Dr. Paul Pruyser of the Menninger Foundation was talking to a group of ministers. He really set us back on our heels. "Other professionals are envious of you," he said. "No one else has the freedom of *initiative* which you have. *We* have to wait until they come to us. You have the holy privilege of going to them." [8]

Sure some people will be defensive. Of course some folks won't respond. But occasionally a man or woman secretly wants help and inwardly will be grateful to the pastor who knocks on the door—not to manipulate but to offer concrete help. I've talked a number of men into counseling. Sometimes I've been devious and said things like, "I think your wife would be less anxious and progress faster if you'd come with her. She needs your encouragement." Sometimes it works.

The secular counselor may sit in his office. He may help a lot of people. He may say that you can only help those who want help (meaning those who have enough ego strength and money to come). Or he may honestly wish he had opportunity to go out into the homes. But he doesn't. The pastor *does* have the authority of divine initiative. "I came to seek and save the lost," said our Lord. In his name we have the right to go and offer help.

There's another way to take initiative. That's to work with doctors, attorneys, and other pastors. Let them know what you're doing. Talk with pastors and priests to develop a cooperative strategy. Mention that you are forming a group and need another couple. Invite referrals. Ask for supervisory help from a clinical psychologist and work with couples from his family counseling service.

Intake Interviews and Contracting

Even in his office, a pastor works differently than a marriage counselor. The genius of the pastoral role is his flexibility. He is a general practitioner. A woman walks into the office claiming she doesn't like the flower arrangement on the altar. Before long she may confide that her husband has moved out. A man calls on the phone and makes an appointment because he "needs to talk to somebody." The wise pastor goes slow until he discovers whether the stress involves the loss of a job, the death of the man's mother, or a breakdown in the home. It takes a while to get the feel of a situation. With marriage problems it often requires two or three sessions with one person before the other is ready to become involved. Deeply confidential material may come out in private that will never come out in the group. Sometimes an acute problem can be resolved within two or three sessions, and there is no need for further involvement. The value of having a group available is that it provides a method of treatment in the back of the pastor's mind.

Referrals are a completely different ball game. A great deal of preliminary work has already been done. When Dr. Harris sent a couple, he had completed a medical examination and a shrewd emotional evaluation of the woman. Sometimes he had observed the man as well. When an attorney referred, he generally could send both man and woman. He had weighed the likelihood for reconciliation. I was able to structure referrals on a more businesslike basis than I could with members of the congregation. With referrals, I began to use a brief "intake form" (Appendix C). It enabled me to conduct a brief interview, gain quick factual information, and determine a direct strategy for helping them.

From the very beginning, the pastor initiates a process known technically as "contracting." Contracting is not writing a document; it is developing a relationship. Key questions are: *Why did you come? Why did you come now?*

Why did you come to me? These questions begin to pin-point the problem. They begin to determine what the couple expects of the counselor and what the counselor expects of them. Most pastors are particularly deficient at this point, leaving a lot of things "up in the air." For example, a couple might indicate that they have come because they can't talk to each other anymore. Why now? They might say that their last child has married and left home. They feel that if they can't rediscover each other, there's no point in continuing the relationship. It is also helpful for the pastor to ask. "Why me?" They might say that they thought maybe the church could help them, or that it was a last gasp before divorce, or that they had heard that you (the pastor) had helped some friends of theirs. Their answers will show some expectations. Then the contracting moves into a discussion of the kind of treatment-growth program which seems warranted.

Conclusion: Summary of Structural Values

There might be some free spirits accustomed to human relations encounters or sensitivity experiences who would demand a more laissez-faire structure. But it must be remembered that we are talking about people who are really hurting, whose anxiety level is so high that they are already about to "jump off the bridge." For healing dynamics to take place, there must be clean, clearly defined boundaries. The leader must be in charge. The program must be carefully negotiated. The structures must be understood. The group counseling design is meant to provide a consistent, supportive environment with a minimum of "external" anxieties. We want to work on internal tensions and interpersonal relationships without additional stress or confusion. In this respect, the group is like a temporary hospital in which people are removed for a couple of hours from their regular surroundings and relieved for a time from normal stress.

That is why structural guidelines as size, time per session, duration of therapy, place, commonality of pain, personality make-up of the group, and continual contracting are essential. If the kind of process is to occur which is restorative of broken relationships, then the setting must be an environment which will enable maximum healing to take place.

Chapter IV
Group Process

Group process is exceedingly difficult, and in some ways impossible, to describe. How can a writer convey a tear in a man's eye or a seemingly endless moment of silence when something happens? Those who have written verbatims and process notes from individual counseling sessions know how difficult *that* task is. Even in the individual reporting, it is difficult if not impossible to convey feelings and nonverbal expressions. The dynamics of a group of ten people working for two hours are not increased arithmetically but rather are multiplied geometrically. The leader in the room does not fully know what is going on—so many things are happening at once. No wonder written materials are two-dimensional, cardboard efforts to communicate experience that is essentially noncommunicable.

This argument is not a cop out. It is not a retreat from a stringent task. Recently I participated in a group workshop under the highly trained and sensitive Father George Dougherty of St. Thomas Aquinas Seminary in Dubuque, Iowa. He made extensive use of psychodrama as a way of opening up and observing feelings within the group. I was so moved by the experience and saw such excellent possibilities for application in our marriage counseling groups, that I asked where I could get my hands on some descriptive material. He grinned and asked me why I didn't write up a descriptive account of what had happened within our group in the three weeks together. I was appalled. I could not even describe meaningfully what happened in the total group for an individual session.

I have previously referred to the exciting work which Chaplain C. L. Bruninga is doing with couples at the state hospital in Norwich, Connecticut. He indicated in a professional journal that he was trying to prepare some tapes that would describe significant moments in group experience. He hoped thereby to equip others for group leadership. I wrote to him asking about his tapes. His letter of reply indicates the problem:

> The attempt to develop training tapes on the group marriage counseling process, after hundreds of hours of work handed in, ended in failure. The usual problem being that we could not find brief enough sections of the tape which illustrate the therapeutic process.

Dr. Kenneth Mitchell, head of the division of psychiatry and religion at the Menninger Foundation, indicated in a recent conversation the immensity of the descriptive problems. He mentioned that Bach and Wyden's book, *The Intimate Enemy,* was as imaginative and helpful as anything written. The book tries to open up for the reader the real feel of a marriage therapy process. In spite of the fact that the book is based on a wealth of experience, contains huge amounts of interaction material, and was written by a professional and highly skilled journalistic writer, it still leaves the reader feeling "once removed" from what really happened. I found myself wanting desperately to sit in on a session and see for myself.

But even observing groups in action is not as easy as it might seem. Mr. Orville Shoemaker, marriage group counselor at the Prairie View Hospital, reminded me that when another person enters a group, it becomes, in fact, a different group. In a technical article entitled, "The Effect of Observers on the Process of Group Therapy," Doctors Bloom and Dobie review the literature on observers. They realize that outsiders or newcomers or observers affect the group experience, but then argue that these intrusions or modifications can be used by the leader. In particular, these men tried to make therapeutic use of resistance and transference. But the point is that the group experience is actually different with an observer present.[1]

Most group therapists and group counselors have begun flying by the seat of their pants. Not only has it been true for me, a normally trained pastor in an average church in Kansas, but it generally is true of specialized and professional therapists. At some point or other, a person simply has to begin.

The Necessity to Begin

Some would like to wait until they have the right theory of personality development. But theories are like theologies, and a preacher would never begin to preach if he waited until his total theology was intact. Besides, effective help is currently being given within the context of many diverse theoretical orientations. Dr. Fern J. Azima argues:

It seems relevant to note that it is the therapist's personality and idiosyncratic background that dictates his

choice among the various group techniques. The decision
to use one or other of the therapeutic approaches is not
based solely upon theoretical grounds. Some individuals
are "by nature" able to utilize a spontaneous interactional
approach. Some are inclined to be passive leaders, others
more authoritarian. There is little doubt that the conduc-
tor's own repertoire is a crucial influence on the symphony
and style of production. . . . *The surprise is that patients
do get better by what apparently theoretically are widely
divergent methods.*[2]

The point is that with desperate people crying out all
about us, we ought to be up and about it. As Hulme, the
Lutheran pastoral counselor, suggests:

We have finally come to the end of the referral obses-
sion. The clergyman is becoming less frightened about
"getting over his head." He has had enough involvement
with psychiatrists, psychologists and caseworkers to dispel
the illusion that these other professions hold the panacea.
Too many people have returned from their stint with these
others to ask again for the pastor's help. . . . Seeing
other professionals more realistically, the pastor has more
confidence to carry on even if it seems only that he is
muddling through.[3]

Of course, this argument is not to be taken as a way of
avoiding opportunities for professional growth. Some sug-
gestions for training will be offered in chapter V. Nevertheless, every leader and every group is different. A counselor
has, at some point or another, simply had to start.

If you've had an experience of God's grace and see
something of what the impact of a group can be, experiment in gathering a few kindred spirits into your home
or church house. If you are a minister, "take a chance."[4]

Categories of Group Process: A New Environment

When Dr. C. F. Menninger first conceived the idea of a psychiatric clinic and hospital in Topeka, Kansas, one of his prime motivations was to create a healing environment. At both East and West Campuses, considerable attention is paid to the grounds—trees, flowers, pools, shaded walkways, bird houses, and feeding stations. He was convinced that a new, warm, friendly, and beautiful environment provides a nonthreatening context in which a person starts to put the pieces back together again. So it is with marriage group counseling. Much tragedy springs from early homelife—broken relationships, grating conflict, sexual fears, and guilt-ridden anxieties. One woman, for example, remembered in technicolor the time her mother struggled to disarm her father. He was attempting to shoot the mother and children with a shotgun. Childhood agony continues and surfaces within the marriage. Learned ways of fighting have become established patterns. Confused roles have been defended and stabilized. A stoney silence has surrounded certain subjects. A new environment is necessary for change to take place.

A group adheres to the principle that people can share openly and in confidence feelings and thoughts which are their own. Honesty is the order of the day. It's OK to feel what you feel. I have seen anger or resentment wiggle on the floor like a snake. Such open expressions are difficult in social groups, but in the treatment group, protection is built in. The counselor provides this protection as he helps the groups objectify and reflect on what happens. The group itself provides protection: members will come to the defense of one unjustly treated or too threatened by a confrontation.

Many have argued, and I think rightly so, that the group is like the family. This fact makes group counseling all the more appropriate for marital problems. One woman said that she "couldn't get over just being invited into the minister's home." Some quickly saw traits of their mothers, fathers, sisters, brothers, husbands, and wives in the personalities of others in the room.

> In the family . . . unsuccessful patterns of relating have been learned. The group method seizes upon this understanding and is based on the expectancy that, in a situation similar to that of the family, a matrix is available for re-education and for correction of unhealthy and conflictive styles of relating.[5]

Most people have never experienced the environment of acceptance. If one were to think in Tillich's concept of the event of Grace, it could be said correctly that the group sets the stage for the event of Grace. The session is not just another meeting. "The emotional climate of a therapeutic group affords the freedom with others to be what one is, to feel what one feels, and to communicate what one really feels and thinks." [6] Within the group, Tillich's words that "you are accepted" become an experienced reality. The covenant nature of the group is like that of a trustworthy family. Family confidences are kept. What comes out in the group is the property of the group.

We are continually trying to get people to own up to their feelings instead of talking about what other people (especially their mates) think and feel. Here is an environment where it's OK to have feelings: anger or guilt or anxiety. To use the concept of Thomas Harris, "I'm OK, You're OK."

In twisted family life there is a continual effort to make someone else change. Criticism by one is countered by defensiveness in the other. Many a young man, for example, figures that the only problem is his wife. If she'd only warm up a little bit there would be no problem, and so he refuses to get involved in a counseling situation. The woman, on the other hand, makes counter demands such as, "If he would only show a little consideration around the house, maybe I wouldn't be so cold." As long as each hides his own feelings and demands that the other person change, there is a standoff and things go from bad to worse. Dr. Paul Tournier puts his finger on this point in saying,

> As long as man is accused by other people, he defends himself; it is a universal reflex. This defensive attitude prevents him from "coming to himself" and undergoing a moral experience. In the belief that they are leading him toward such an experience, they are in fact leading him away from it. But as soon as other people, instead of casting stones at him, recognize that in the perspective of the heart they are as guilty as he, he accuses himself, he repents and undergoes that moral experience which the Gospel calls salvation. So where others are concerned: total absence of responsibility. Where we ourselves are concerned: total responsibility.[7]

Not only does the new environment provide a climate of acceptance during that one evening a week, but this warmth also radiates into regular family life during the week. The oasis furnishes the fresh clear water of freedom to be oneself and to accept one's mate. People fill up their canteens and later drink from them in their own homes. One woman in her evaluation wrote, "Even if Larry and I aren't together all the time like I used to want, I know he loves me, and when we *are* together, we both are more peaceful and talk more about real things. Sometimes we are quiet together."

When St. Paul wrote about "justification by grace" (Romans 3:24, Ephesians 2:8), he meant that we are accepted in our *being* rather than in our doing. A group may not agree with a person's action patterns, but his personhood is accepted. He has a right to be. Our American society awards gold medals for accomplishment, but the new environment offers a kind of mediated grace in which a person is recognized for just being a person.

> Man cannot exist at all without recognition, without being recognized by others, without rejoicing in recognition himself. . . . But it is a fundamental misconception for him to think that he can extract recognition and establish his claim for recognition through what he does— through his work instead of his being.[8]

This distinction is clearly St. Paul's contrast between justification by works and justification by grace. The group provides a setting in which a person has important reality just by his existence, by his own and by the groups' acknowledgement of his personhood.

The environment is more than a hospital; it is also a hothouse. Not only are we trying to heal wounds of the past; we are also trying to nurture a growth for the future. Group life ought to ground a person into elemental aspects of basic trust and love. It should set in motion the dynamics of a positive love relationship that can continue to develop. Dr. Howard J. Clinebell, Jr., speaking to a seminar on pastoral care sponsored by the Methodist Hospital in Peoria, Illinois, stated that the church ought not limit itself to the "medical model."[9] We are interested in healing broken persons and broken marriages, but we are concerned with more than that. We want an openness to the future. We work for fresh beginnings. Trust and hope and love are dynamic terms in which a person or a marriage is in process of becoming. Clinebell urges us to use the model of growth.

The kingdom of God involves growth. Jesus used the parable of the seeds and the parable of the leaven. Nowhere is the concept of growth more vital than in marriage relationships. So, in the counseling group, we want an environment where old hurts can be healed. But we also want a setting which will start growing healthy relationships which can survive, even flourish, in the real world.

A Dialogical Community

No society has ever had more talk and less communication than ours. Through TV, radio, and press, the production and conveyance of words has reached astronomical proportions. We are bombarded by words. Yet in business, government, and in marriage, people complain about a "breakdown in communications." What does it mean when a couple with college educations, both of whom are quite verbal, even loquacious, say that they have no communication? They complain that they can't talk to each other anymore. Although it is almost a cliché now, the failure of communications within the home seems to be the rootage problem, from which so many other difficulties spring.

Reuel Howe, leaning heavily on Martin Buber but sifting his thoughts through his own interpersonal experiences, has written the extremely helpful book, *Miracle of Dialogue.* In his book, Howe defines communication as a "meeting of meaning." [10] It is false to assume that just because people can talk they can communicate. The meeting of meaning requires an openness, a receptivity, and a vulnerability. I have just returned from a three-day meeting of ministers that was designed to be discussion oriented. On the first afternoon we talked for four solid hours. The following afternoon several of the men were hostile. In fact, they were flushed-faced-angry! They were upset with the discussion leader. Finally, one man blurted out, "Yesterday, you didn't even hear what we were trying to say!" In so many marriages (maybe in all to a greater or lesser degree) husbands and wives are crying out, "You aren't even hearing what I'm trying to say!"

In the counseling group, we try to hear what others are saying. We try to meet at the "meaning" level. We try to reach across the male-female feeling chasm and, to use Buber's phrase, "experience the other side." One man wrote in his evaluation, "I thought I had been listening to my wife all along, but I found that actually I was turning her off. When I really began to try to understand what she was feeling, I realized that I experienced those very same feelings." A common problem area in many homes is the man who comes home after too much social stimulus. He wants to withdraw. He encounters his wife who is lonely from the day's isolation (or preoccupation with little children). He wants quiet. She needs to ventilate. Couples have desperate fights in that context. She hates him for hiding behind a newspaper or gluing himself in front of an "idiot tube." He thinks she is a bitch for "yelling at him when he walks in the front door." Over and over again in a group, feelings of frustration are registered for the first time. One man finally was able to say clearly, "All I want is a bottle of beer and a moment of quiet while I regroup my feelings. Hearing you fixing supper in the kitchen and knowing you are near really makes me feel good. After a few minutes I'll be able to talk." That night his wife actually "heard" him. She agreed to let him alone for an hour; in return he goes into the kitchen, drinks a cup of coffee, and visits while she finishes fixing supper.

Sometimes a woman, in the "meeting of meaning" has been known to blurt out to her husband, "All I want is for you to show me that you think my housework is important. That taking care of the kids is important. I just want you to act like *I'm important* and to tell me you love me."

Another woman was unusually perceptive. Her husband was going through severe business stress. He came home each evening and fell on the sofa in a depressed mood. She decided to lie down on the sofa beside him. She put her arms around him and held him for an hour in near total silence. Some months later, his anxiety diminished, and he no longer needed that intense kind of support. She went with him through a dark valley, and they both came out of it together. T. S. Eliot in *The Cocktail Party* writes:

> Hell is oneself
> Hell is alone, the other figures in it
> Merely projections. There is nothing to escape from
> And nothing to escape to. One is always alone.[11]

No one experiences a lonelier hell than a husband or wife who feels that his mate does not know his feelings, understand his needs, or care about those things that are important to him.

Of the variety of groups with their different styles, those that are alive are always dialogical. This fact was brought home to me when I read about the "listening groups" which the Reverend Robert A. Edgar has formed in New York

City. Dr. Edgar, pastor of the Central Presbyterian Church on Manhattan Island, realizes how lonely so many couples in his congregation are, especially couples new to the city and to his church. He makes a special effort to have only emotionally stable people. Instead of studying a book, people simply share one another's thoughts and feelings. The groups are needed because, he says, in New York "no one really listens to another—not even when they are ill or near death. . . . They usually nod in agreement that few people experience relationships in which they can be truly trusting and honest." [12] The groups meet in homes or apartments on a bimonthly basis. The pastor meets with them for a few weeks to make sure they begin listening to what others are saying and feeling. It is really a laboratory in listening.

"In every conversation between two people, there are always at least six people present:
    What each person says is two;
    What each person meant to say are two more;
    What each person understood the other to say are two more." [13]

Over thirty-five such groups in two parishes prove that wholesome and valuable interpersonal needs have been met. Of special interest to us is the fact that:

Groups composed of couples have proved to be the most productive. Many husbands and wives have the rare privilege of not only "hearing" each other for the first time, but of being listened to in depth as the group opens the door to continued listening to each other at home. Most couples say they continue the discussion of "what happened" during the evening way past bedtime. Dozens of couples have witnessed to the enriching of their marriage because of the insights coming from their group. Several marriages have actually been saved. Only on one occasion in hundreds and hundreds of meetings has a marriage been threatened. The discussion that evening triggered a domestic squabble that was about to erupt anyway. This, then, opened the way to provide some much needed counseling which led to a healing situation.[14]

Why is this dialogical commodity so precious? Because it is so expensive! In the New Testament, the verb is *dialogizomai,* and it means to bring together different reasons. The word implies tension. It's hard work. Most people have the mistaken idea that the mere desire to say something is enough. It is an act of love to listen, to get involved, to care. Listening opens oneself up as much as talking. It takes work; it takes soul.

> Dialogue is to love, what blood is to the body. When the flow of blood stops, the body dies. When dialogue stops, love dies and resentment and hate are born. But dialogue can restore a dead relationship. Indeed, this is the miracle of dialogue; it can bring relationship into being, and it can bring into being once again a relationship that has died. There is only one qualification to these claims for dialogue: it must be mutual and proceed from both sides, and the parties to it must persist relentlessly.[15]

One of the fascinating things about group experience is that people gain a growing insight into the meaning of nonverbal communications. People, of course, send off signals all the time. Learning to read them and to use them therapeutically helps the counselor tremendously. It is well to remember that communication is like an iceberg, with the verbals analogous to the exposed part. Most is under water. The analogy breaks down however in this sense: often the verbal comments are confused and distorted whereas the nonverbal communications are more authentically related to actual feelings. Throughout the United States today, all sort of work is being conducted using nonverbal techniques. Some approaches emphasize music, dance, touch, expressive art forms, role play, or psychodrama. Undoubtedly some of this emphasis is faddish and narrow, but the general practitioner can learn from them and at least become sensitive to body position, use of hands, head, eyes, and feet. For example, a leader might observe a man sitting with legs crossed and arms folded and simply say, "Joe, you seem sort of closed off from the group tonight—like you're kind of walling us out."

Recently in one of our groups, a young woman told how upset she had been a few years ago when her husband's best friend told her their marriage would never last. She said it made her furious, but she never said anything to the man. She just left him alone. I asked her to go to the other side of the room, pretend that I was that "friend," walk toward me as in a "corridor," and do whatever she felt like doing to me. I told her she could hit me, or kick me, or spit on me, or hug me—whatever she felt like doing. I stood, relaxed, and she began very slowly to walk toward me. About a yard away (arm's length), she stopped. She just stood there in silence, totally without visible emotion. Finally I asked if that was all she was going to do. And she said yes. Now as this woman's pastor, I knew that she had an ulcer. I knew that she could talk for hours without saying anything. Her real feelings were always hidden, or perhaps more accurately, held back. I was not too surprised when she came into my study the next day and told me that she had wakened during the night and burst out into tears. She roused her husband and poured out feelings of hurt and anger and loneliness like she never had before in her life. They talked and hugged and kissed and cried for three hours. In the "corridor" she had seen herself more clearly than ever before.

Dialogue can begin without words—before words are able to be spoken. That is, people can sometimes begin to talk with their hands or bodies before they are able to start talking with their mouths. Early in a group's formation, we have had a night for describing our marriages graphically. Couples have brought old magazines, paste, paper, crayons, pipe cleaners, buttons, etc. Each person sprawled on the floor making a collage or picture which described his marriage as he saw it. We spent the next hour talking about the pictures and what they were trying to say. It was dialogical. People had been invited to reveal themselves, and they responded by opening themselves. It was a "meeting of meaning."

A Caring Community

A group in the life of the church or under the leadership of a pastor or lay counselor can draw heavily upon the caring, concerned dimension of love. I believe, at this point, we have an advantage over the secular agency. Theologically, we believe that God loves us; at our deepest core we know that God in Christ has an unconditional positive regard for men (*Christus pro nobis*). Within the group, some people will experience for the first time that people care—and that God cares.

Prayer itself opens up an ocean of caring. The Yokefellow program calls for a half-hour period of personal meditation each day as a part of the discipline. We incorporated into that plan the request that each person pray for each other by name during that time of meditation and prayer. Even those who did not believe in God were asked simply to remember each person with good will. Across the months we experienced tornadoes and hail, the loss of property and crops, births, deaths, sickness, accidents, divorces filed, sick children, teen-agers in trouble, etc. Through it all, there was the constant, sturdy support of daily, personal prayer within a caring fellowship. Couples who originally said they had no friends, who thought that no one cared whether they lived or died, now knew that there were some who prayerfully followed their ups and downs. Early in the program people were late to meetings; as time went on, they came early. Friendships developed; women called each other during the week to see how the kids were; men inquired with real seriousness about business, sales, crops.

We learned to touch each other, not in dramatic ways, but in meaningful moments. We inevitably shook hands as we arrived and left. Sometimes the women would hug each other. Erik Erikson has written somewhere that the "first step in the relationship of trust is touch." Our most healing experience of touch was the concluding prayer circle each evening. It seemed very natural to stand in a tightly knit circle holding hands. If someone had revealed himself without reserve, it was a good time to be supportive. One evening in the middle of the session, a young woman left the room in tears. Another woman slipped out, put her arm around her, and eventually brought her back into the room. In our prayer circle, I was able to say, "Mary has shed some holy tears tonight, and we love her." Affirmation flowed through our hands like electricity through a circuit. Dr. Paul Pruyser of Menninger's has written an article on the "Master Hand" in which he urges the use of the symbolic touch of the pastor. Mr. Pruyser feels that people have a deep need to be blessed. It seemed to me that as I initiated the circle, it was a kind of shepherd's blessing. But it was more than that, for it was the touch of the whole group. The group actually assumes pastoral functions. The touch means self-giving, empathy, concern. Dr. Pruyser writes that "some people at some times wish that someone would put a benevolent hand on their heads for just one moment." This is a great gift which pastors and only pastors can bestow.[16] That act can be performed on occasion and is experienced to some extent by the group in the circle of hands.

People in the group inevitably want to talk about God. They are concerned about faith, forgiveness, love. We define prayer as total honesty, honesty to oneself, with others, and before God. Most persons in the group begin to perceive that the experience of acceptance in the group is part and parcel of an even greater acceptance by God the Father. I have a bundle of books available for those who want to read. Some of Tillich's sermons on forgiveness and acceptance begin to speak to them. Scriptures about God's love begin to make sense. In short, the couples are never quite sure whether the love of the group has brought them closer to the love of God or whether the love of God has brought them into a sharing community; but most are convinced that there is a relationship. One man learned to say "I love you" to his wife and to God at the same moment of his life.

Part of the caring ministry of the group deals with present trials and tribulations. Sometimes a crisis causes the love level to rise to new heights. The case history of Jim and Mary is an example. Their marriage had blossomed during the group experience. Mary was off tranquilizers, and Jim was confident and relaxed. They were expecting a baby, and everyone was giving them plenty of good-natured ribbing. As they left the house one Wednesday evening, we called out the back door, urging them to let us know as soon as the baby arrived. The call came at midnight on Thursday. It said, "Please come to the hospital right away." The baby was stillborn. It was a lonely couple who prayed with their doctor and pastor that night. The baby was buried the following Monday with some from the group present at the graveside. Others dropped by the house. The following Wednesday night, Jim and Mary were among the first to arrive at the group meeting. I've seldom seen a room so full of love.

Caring is not all of therapy, but it is a pillar of the structure. Dr. Karl Menninger, in *Love Against Hate,* has written, "If we can love enough . . . this is the touchstone. This is the key to the entire therapeutic program of the modern psychiatric hospital. . . . Love is the medicine for the sickness of the world." [17]

The Confessional Fellowship

As has been indicated earlier, consoling motherly love, though essential, is not enough. Glasser keeps the balance when he points not only to the need to love and be loved, but also to the need to feel worthwhile to oneself and others. I have counseled scores of couples and many individuals who had lost their self-respect. Guilt feelings run rampant through troubled marriages. One psychiatrist once told me that 90 percent of his patients had trouble with guilt.

In an accepting, dialogical fellowship of love, much material is shared that is of a confessional nature. The group can provide a "confessional" more vital than a priestly sacrament or a parson's study. Without any doubt, the work of getting rid of guilt is a key to any program of therapy, and most especially in marriage counseling.

There was a time when people spoke of guilt feelings rather than guilt. Words like inhibition and free expression were used instead of conscience and atonement. Empathy with feelings was thought to be more pastoral than concern for responsible action. But today, fatherly care, to use Fromm's concept, is regaining a rightful place. There is danger of identifying healing with consolation. Dr. O. Hobart Mowrer of the University of Illinois is strongly influenced by Alcoholics Anonymous. He perceives open confession as the very heart and center of healing. He speaks of real guilt as resulting from tangible acts of a man's behavior which are done in violation of his conscience. This misbehavior is concealed from the "significant others" in his world in order to avoid the pain of disapproval, punishment, or rejection. Healing or cleansing consists of an honest disclosure of oneself to others and ultimately to the significant others followed by all possible repair of injuries.[18] And who, incidentally, is more significant than one's husband or wife?

What happens in a counseling group? It seems to me that there are two levels of confession. One is the revealing of a specific act. For example, one night a young man told the group he didn't come the previous week because he had been furious with his wife, had beat her up, and then felt ashamed of himself. The group listened, permitted him freely to express his anger and guilt, listened to his wife tearfully reveal her shame, and then talked about appropriate ways of handling anger. The session provided the milieu in which he was able to say, "I'm sorry," and she was able to accept that without shaming him. Neither he nor she had to grovel in the dirt to move closer together.

The trouble with Mowrer's thesis, however, is that it is too simple. The implications of his writings are that (a) someone does an act which violates his conscience and (b) when he tells a counselor or pastor and the significant others, he will be free again. But the problem is much more complicated than that. In almost every instance with couples where there was shame and guilt, confession had already been made to the pastor or doctor and to the husband or wife. (When it had a repentance dimension, some healing had begun.) But so many of the people still felt unworthy, unacceptable. They felt a social alienation from society and from the church.

I remember in particular Jeanette, age twenty-seven. Jeanette was adopted by a single, professional woman and thus never had a father in her home. She had polio, with a resultant curvature of the spine. At sixteen she became pregnant out of marriage. She released her baby for adoption. Now, married and with a child in the home, she still had great feelings of shame, unacceptability, lack of worth —even though her husband, her mother, and, in the course of the sessions, the group knew about all these experiences. But she had a desperate need for social (and religious) reassurance that she was OK. Confession for her was a revelation of her shame, her incompleteness, to a social grouping rather than a disclosure of an act to an offended individual.

In group sharing, like confession in the early church, a person shares present thoughts and feelings as well as past deeds. Not only were acts of individual misbehavior revealed, but feelings (the so-called unacceptable feelings) such as fear and hate and shame were confessed. One night in one of our groups we were talking about fear. We discussed fear of life and fear of death. Marjean, a plain woman of forty-eight years had come to the group at her doctor's urging. She was often in bed for three days at a time with severe headaches and depression. On this particular evening, she began to talk quietly about a night in the hospital when she wanted to die. It was the first honest revelation on her part. She said that her prayers were meaningless and wooden, that her pain was so great she thought she could not stand it. She said, "I know it is a terrible sin, but I wanted to die that night." This spark of honesty ignited a small fire. Soon several were talking about times they planned to crash their cars into a concrete buttress or to take a bottle of pills. They agreed that at such times they were so depressed that they could neither pray nor communicate with people. One said that God was totally remote, and it seemed that nobody cared. George, a strong, suntanned man in his forties, seeming secure and confident, listened intently. He scarcely said a word. Nobody but his wife and I knew about his fears of committing suicide. As the conversation neared its close, George simply said, "I've felt that way sometimes, too." Real healing took place for him in that brief confession.

Most of the "gutty" confessions occurred in individual pastoral sessions or with the couple privately. Some confessed privately as new "rocks" of guilt were turned over to the light and "creepy" things were exposed. In the group, people obliquely alluded to the drinking, the infidelities, the sexual unhappiness, the jail sentence. Much of the time they shared feelings of fear, loneliness, and insecurity.

Usually people in a group reveal a general sense of discouragement over being the kind of persons they are. They are filled with worthlessness, emptiness. They have a low self-image. The group is helpful because some significant persons are there—the mate, friends, and the pastor or counselor. Not only are unacceptable actions confessed, but also unacceptable thoughts and feelings are shared. When a person opens himself to the group and is *accepted* he experiences a *reentry* into society. The group provides a microcosm of acceptance by both society and the church.

A Cadre of Accountability

Respect is earned. Fatherly love pulls a person toward the possibility of achievement. A boy strives to gain his father's respect and thereby establish his own self-esteem. Self-respect and self-esteem can be lost, but they also can be regained. One key marital problem is that couples often lack common goals. They experience little sense of attainment. Sometimes there is so little "togetherness" in accomplishing anything that just to keep an appointment with a counselor is a victory. One couple who drove forty miles each way on Wednesday night said it was the first time in years that they had done anything together on a weekly basis. A couple who fulfills the disciplines of the group takes infant steps in learning to walk with their heads up.

Furthermore, the group holds individuals accountable. When a couple is struggling with a problem, someone will inevitably ask how they are getting along. Finances, for example, are often a difficulty because of conflict and irresponsibility. Separate living expenses, divorce proceedings, and attorney fees may have added to the pile of bills. But once the couple decides on a plan of action and actually begins to nibble away at the mountain of obligations, they begin to feel that they are pulling together. They are accomplishing something; they are being responsible. They may even hear someone else say, "Gee, you two are an inspiration to us—I hope we can do as well."

John tipped over his truck one night when he was drunk. He often came home in the wee hours with "four sails in the wind." He decided one night to quit drinking. Without badgering him at all, members of the group, from time to time, would simply ask how he was getting along. Since it was his idea, his goal, it brought him considerable self-respect to be able to say, "Fine, no problem."

Even sexual improvement was discussed to some extent. Usually it was euphemized, but it was real, nonetheless. A man would say that he had rearranged his sales district so he could be home nearly every night. Or a woman would say that, for the first time in her married life, she had agreed to leave the children with a sitter and take a weekend vacation with her husband.

One of our most difficult counselees was a man who was immature in his personality development. I should never have allowed him in the group. He was a camel so slow that sometimes the caravan scarcely moved. His wife worked hard at her job and then came home to take care of the house and the baby. He slept until nearly noon, did some odd jobs and a little part-time farming. One night he said that he had thought about looking for a job, and the group really pushed him. They told him that his wife was working too hard and he wasn't working hard enough. They began to ask him how he was getting along in his job hunting. They got angry with him, disgusted with him; but they still cared for him. To my knowledge he still has only worked part-time here and there, but he has expanded his farming operations, and his wife claims that he is helping her more. One thing is for sure, the group held him consistently accountable for his efforts. And they did this without rejecting him as a person; in fact, their very concerns were a form of acceptance.

To conclude, group process is still impossible to describe. Neither word pictures nor diagram arrows tell the story. Testimony is interesting but not descriptive. Hopefully the principles which have been delineated in this chapter will be guidelines for observation. Apparently there is no substitute for immediate experience and personal encounter. I know of no one who is doing significant group counseling with married couples who did not take a deep breath and plunge into the deeps.

Chapter V
The Pastor as Group Counselor

Reasons for Seeing a Pastor

Availability

Why would people come to a minister or priest in the first place? I'm sure that there are a myriad of reasons. Sometimes it is simply his availability. In countless small communities across the country, there is a total lack of agencies for family guidance or counseling. How many pastors have had a person express the conviction that there just didn't seem to be anywhere else to go. Even in cities where mental health centers and professional counselors are available, there are sometimes long delays with red tape and waiting lists. Often there is confusion in the minds of troubled people as to the exact kind of help which the agencies provide.

Fear

Mental health facilities, psychiatric centers, and psychiatrists are still frightening to many people. Although we have made tremendous strides in the past three decades in lessening these fears, they still are present. The situation is similar to that which existed with regard to physical illness, doctors, and hospitals some half-century ago. In the days of Dr. Hertzler and *The Horse and Buggy Doctor,* it was not at all unusual for people to refuse to go to the hospital because they felt it was the place you went when you were going to die. Today countless people who readily accept medical help for physical illness are nevertheless highly resistent to professional help for emotional illness. Rapid progress is being made, however, and it might be said that ministers, priests, and rabbis are playing a tremendous role in breaking down these fears. Pastors are continually referring people to psychiatrists for help, giving them reassurance during their therapy, and helping to interpret the experience to families and friends. Recently Mr. Red Pratt, public information officer for the Menninger Foundation, indicated in conversation that a large percentage of the patients at Menninger's come by referral from ministers.

Nevertheless, given the lack of availability of nearby mental health facilities and the fear that many people still have concerning psychiatric help, millions of people turn to their spiritual advisors. The wise pastor carefully selects those he can help and works competently with them. Then he joins with others in developing sources of referral for those who are beyond his time or ability.

Expense

Of course money, or the lack of it, plays a part too, and we might as well face it. Medical and counseling fees are expensive, generally are not covered by insurance, and often are justification for delaying requests for help. Now, there are two ways of looking at this fee problem. One

97

way is to see the pastor as a cheap counselor who is available for those who can't or won't pay for first class help. A few counselors who are trying to make a living on a fee basis have, somewhat defensively, categorized ministers as "Dear Abbys" with a Bible and a collar. Some ministers have degraded themselves with the "they can't afford a professional, so they came to me" self-image. But in all reality, many people are flocking to spiritual leaders with great expectations. They often give us greater status than we deserve. It's true that some people don't have much money, but that provides us with an opportunity for services that few other professional people have. We dare not let the nature of our salaries undermine our confidence in our calling. We are highly trained and experienced professional people whose time and involvement have high value. We do ourselves and our calling a great injustice if we sell ourselves short.

Should a fee be charged? From the medical and professional counseling world comes a strong yes. Most psychiatrists argue that payment for services is an aspect of therapy itself. People value highly what they must pay for; they value lowly what is free. There is a deep emotional need to say thank you. In a materialistic society, we say thank you with money. People feel guilty for receiving help until they have had a way to reimburse. Besides, people will feel more committed and will work harder if they are paying each week. The law of Moses required people who had been healed to report to the priests and give a gift to God. Jesus said to the ten lepers, "Go and show yourselves to the priests" (Luke 17:14). That admonition carried with it the demand to offer a sacrifice in the temple.

Those of us in the ministry or priesthood have not seen our work traditionally on a fee basis. We expect the people of our churches to pay their tithes and offerings and thereby support our total ministry. No pastor would charge a fee for making a hospital call or for going to a home where tragedy has occurred or for talking to a teen-ager who is groping with a vocational choice. Unless a church has a formal counseling service in connection with the parish, there is seldom a fee for pastoral counseling.

Still, group counseling requires a tremendous investment of time with a handful of people. It requires a unique kind of depth involvement. Many of the couples may be un-churched or from another parish. They provide little sup-port for the pastor or his church. Their involvement may be careless because no financial demands are made upon them. They may feel guilty for sponging off the goodwill of others.

We tried a number of approaches. When testing was done in connection with the Yokefellow Prayer Therapy program, each person paid his $20.00 fee. Couples were encouraged to support their churches and were urged to give special gifts to my congregation's budget. Some gave more to their own churches than before. A few of our own members began to tithe in gratitude for the experience. Some people did nothing at all. For the most part, this latter group gained least from counseling.

I toyed with the idea of charging a dollar per week for each thousand dollars annual income, with the money to go to the church. I considered a fee for nonmembers, but it seemed unwise to distinguish between members and non-members. So I backed off of fees altogether. Whichever way the pastor-counselor goes, however, he should clearly indicate to the couples that they have a financial obligation to support the work. They will be shortchanging themselves and undercutting the ministries of the church if they fail to do so.

Trust

Some people simply come to the minister or priest because they believe he has integrity. I am convinced that people place a tremendous level of confidence in a "man of God." They trust him. Some know him and trust him. Others trust him because of his office. Still others trust him because of what others say of him or because they are being referred by people they have faith in. Without any question, this level of confidence is one of the pastor's greatest assets.

The pastor is often seen as one who has made firm commitments to God and who seeks to be concerned for the well-being of people. The Christian pastor has, in Christ Jesus, a model and standard for his own life-style, and people sense this reality and are drawn to it.

Get God on His Side

Occasionally one mate or the other will come into the office in order to *get the preacher (or God) on his side in the marital conflict.* It is not unusual for a woman particularly to endeavor to con the minister into helping her "get the old man straightened out." Generally the husband will be highly resistant to talking to the pastor under those conditions. Essentially one of two approaches lies open to the pastor. First, he has freedom, more freedom than anyone else, to go to the husband (or wife) and indicate his impartiality, his concern, and his willingness to help. A sensible pastor can be aggressive without being obnoxious. The other alternative is to work with the one who comes, modifying the ground rules from how to change your mate to how to change yourself. A good counselor can often begin working with the feelings and attitudes of the one who comes.

Confirming a Decision

Some come to their pastor after they have made up their minds to divorce. They want to get his approval or certification that they are doing the right thing. Some Lutheran pastors have particularly emphasized this point. Members of several denominations are taught from childhood that they should not break their marriages without counseling with their priest or minister. It is a dangerous trap for the pastor when a person is wanting "divine" support for his decision, and it is generally not helpful to agree or to disagree with the decision. To propose group counseling can bring a couple up short. It can force them to decide how serious they are about seeking reconciliation. The pastor has strong leverage when he says, "In three weeks we're beginning a marriage counseling group, and it will be precisely the orientation in which you can work through your feelings and decide for yourselves which course of action would be the best for you." Those who had merely wanted an ecclesiastical nod of approval will refuse the involvement; those with actual ambivalence may decide to risk it.

Subconscious Feelings

Some counselors would argue that *the kind of person chosen as counselor would subconsciously indicate in which direction the individual or couple would like to have the matter go.* That is, a couple going to an attorney is more likely subconsciously to hope that the marriage will be dissolved. The couple going to a priest or preacher or rabbi is more likely to be secretly hoping for a reuniting of their

101

love relationship. I cannot substantiate this in any way, but I have talked with attorneys who have said that it is so frustrating for them to achieve any reconciliation that they often don't even try. I know that in my deepest feelings, no matter how hard I try not to show it, I secretly hope the marriage can be saved, i.e. reconstructed in a fresh love relationship. There are professional marriage counselors who publicly take the position that their job is to assist the couple in working through their feelings and that they (the counselors) have absolutely no stake in the outcome. But I have yet to meet a pastor who can quite put it that way. I have long since abandoned the effort to "hold the marriage together," but I work (and pray) with the hope that a new relationship of trust and love can be established. In any event, if it is true that people chose a pastor secretly hoping that he can help them find a new life together, think what tremendous motivation and opportunity this reality gives us! We ought to be grateful and count that influence on the credit side of the ledger.

Why Some People Won't Come

Now of course there will be some people who will not come to a pastor. Resistance being what it is, there are many who will not seek help from anyone. Hulme says that "defensiveness per se is the greatest obstacle to effective pastoral counseling." [1]

Familiarity

But specifically, some will stay away from clergymen for several reasons. Some know him too well. It is difficult to engage in marriage counseling with very close friends and with parishioners with whom one works in an unusually deep relationship. It is not so difficult in group work as it is in individual counseling or conjoint therapy. Members of my finance committee, choir, and administrative board have been in group counseling. Nevertheless some people feel hesitant, and it is not unusual for a couple who are very active in their church to go to another parish or even to a nearby town because they would rather their own pastor didn't know. Sometimes the minister himself would prefer not to be engaged in long term, structured counseling with close friends in the church. Seward Hiltner points out some of the difficulties, even though on occasion the situation may be temporarily restructured to make a relationship with "professional distance" possible for the necessary time of therapy.[2]

Fear of Public Knowledge

Some within the church are afraid of the lack of privacy. The very involvement in family life, which we have claimed as an asset, is sometimes a liability. Some pastors do not have a private study. A familiar car in front of the small country church each week causes some folks to talk. Also, some people wonder if the pastor will make reference, even guarded reference, to their marriage in a sermon. The preacher must keep priestly confidences, avoiding even allusions to counseling situations, in order to keep such fears at a minimum. Recently I visited with a Mennonite pastor who has had three young married couples visiting with him about their marital stress. They trust him completely but are afraid their relatives and friends in the church and community will find out about their troubles. I suggested that he form a "Bible study" group in his own home with those three couples, allowing some time for sharing of scripture and prayer plus time for working through some of their marital hurts and concerns. But it will be difficult to do, and he may need to make referrals.

Authority Figure

Because a clergyman inevitably represents an authority figure, some will not come because they are afraid of being "chewed out," given "preachy advice," or receiving judgmental condemnation. Just as some dependent persons will look to the authority role, so other, more hostile, will avoid it like the plague. Some ministers by their attitude and image actually strengthen these fears. They are pompous, stuffed shirts, and always appear to speak *"ex cathedra."* Reuel Howe writes:

> Too many ministers and teachers reveal a need to be right, a need that keeps them from hearing what their fellow says, which in many instances may be the truth they *really* need to hear. Laymen often state that their ministers do not like to be questioned or challenged and that for this reason they do not feel free to enter into dialogue with them. The lack of dialogue between clergy and laity weakens the church's witness in the world.[3]

Leading a Group: Pastoral Aptitude

I am convinced that those men who are doing good personal counseling can do highly effective group counseling. And I am certain that pastors who are talented in small group process will be extremely rewarded in group counseling. With some aptitude, grace, and training, this magnificent ministry can open up for countless clergymen. It is true, of course, that it is not the style for everyone. It is a pastoral aptitude. Some prophets will be leading marches for racial justice and for peace. Some ministers will have powerful administrative jobs calling for hard, quick decisions. Other preachers will be flaming evangelists, while still others will be brilliant teachers. We are reminded by the Scriptures that

> there are varieties of gifts, but the same Spirit; and there are varieties of service but the same Lord; and there are varieties of working, but it is the same God who inspires them all in every one. . . . And God has appointed in the church first apostles, second prophets, third teachers, then workers of miracles, then healers, helpers, administrators, speakers in various kinds of tongues. (I Cor. 12:4-6, 28)

To work with distressed married couples no doubt requires some spiritual gifts of healing, teaching, and working of miracles. Counseling is not only a craft to be learned but also a gift that has been received.

> Counseling is a skill, but it is also an art. This does not surprise one who is familiar with the witness of the New Testament and its teaching on the gifts of the Spirit. Some individuals unconsciously are healing personalities; they exert a healing influence of which they may be unaware.[4]

Aspects of this healing personality are empathy and patience, flexibility and spontaneity, honesty and integrity.

A pastor, in order to be effective in group counseling, must be dialogical rather than monological, democratic instead of authoritarian. This fact may mean that the pastor will need to share on occasion some of his own anxieties and hurts. I do not mean that he is to use the group for his own therapy—not at all. But he and his wife may need to reveal that they too have lonely times, they too get angry and argue, they too withdraw and pout. In this way the minister joins, if not the company of the desperate, at least the company of the human.

> Revelation does not mean making known data about oneself or exhibiting powers and talents of which one is proud. . . . The dialogical person does not talk about himself, but he does offer out of himself meaning to which his fellows may make free response.[5]

Here are eight tasks of the group leader: (1) He leads group members to look to one another for help. (2) He focuses on the function of the group as a whole (as well as individuals). (3) He understands that leadership is a shared task. (4) He helps each member fulfill his potential contribution. (5) He asks for concretizing and the personal feelings which accompany that kind of "grounding in experience." (6) He helps direct attention on the immediate experience of members. (7) He helps maintain group morale. He recognizes positive feelings. (8) He draws a communication map saying, "Here's where we've been." [6]

For fun I recently glanced through the evaluation forms from several of our groups to see how those subjective comments by involved couples would stack up against professional criteria for group leaders. Here are some of the comments (the question asked was "what did the leader do?").

"He was there."

"The leader kept the group together! He aided people to say what they really thought, instead of what the others would like to hear."

"*Served coffee.* [emphasis theirs] Helped members express feelings. Forced masks off by probing a bit deeper. Set standards of concern, of acceptance, of noncondemnation, of reverence for God for other members to follow in relating to one another."

"He tried to 'follow the wind'—if anyone was hot against a particular problem, he tried to allow him to open up to the group as much as may have been helpful."

"The first few weeks I thought of the leader as just trying to keep the couples together. Later I felt his trying to convey to us the meaning of love of ourselves, life, our spouses, the importance of honesty in working out problems."

"He seemed to be able to see deeper into us than we could understand ourselves. He helped us establish trust."

"He gently led each individual into saying what was really on his mind. Complimented individuals and couples when ideas were presented or noted progress was made."

"Rev. made us feel at ease. He used himself as an example—never claiming to know all the answers. He would open up a topic and then drop out once it got started among the group."

"Asked questions to help the persons find and let out their true feelings."

"Our leader taught us *how* to pray. He encouraged us to open up which was a very hard thing to do. He was a good listener and understands people and *cares*. He gave us the encouragement to explore our minds. Now I can see myself as I really am most of the time."

"He kept his cool."

"He tried to make each one of us feel that our opinions were worthwhile and important. Lots of times he answered our questions with a question. He put us at ease by admitting his own weaknesses. He urged us to pray for each other by name. At first I didn't realize how important this was. Things begin to happen in a person's life when someone prays for them. He challenged some of our ideas and beliefs."

A Wife's Role

It is interesting to try to evaluate my wife's involvement and influence within the groups. In the first group Julia took an active, regular participation. The second year she participated spasmodically. The third year, she was absent from group sessions almost entirely. We gave reasons for all these options, but they were more emotional than rational, more personal than professional. Little did we know then that literature was beginning to spring up highlighting male-female cotherapists. We did not understand the psychic significance of the husband and wife team which is now being used successfully by some psychologists. Many writers in clinical settings are now stressing the value of two counselors, the importance of both male and female orientations being reflected in the leadership, and a certain model quality even when the male psychologist and the female psychologist are not specifically husband and wife.

My wife grasped the need for certain feminine reflections and observations. It is interesting, in the evaluations, how much members of the group (both men and women) seemed to appreciate her presence. She saw herself as a mixture of participant and assistant leader, and on occasion ventilated deep feelings.

As the months wore on, however, my wife's involvement began to cause us some personal problems of our own. As we were to begin our third group, I asked her not to participate. Our four school-age children needed attention and help with studies. Also we had never clearly spelled out our roles between ourselves. She was a participant and yet not a participant. At times she was in the role of leader, yet she was not clearly the leader. She is a strong, effervescent person, and I found myself threatened by her interjections. Undoubtedly the occasional leadership tension within our day-to-day marriage surfaced from time to time in the group situation. In a conversation with Dr. Kenneth Mitchell of the Menninger Foundation, he remarked that tensions of this sort are almost invariably found between cotherapists, even trained male and female psychologists, and even, in a kind of husband-wife interaction, when both cotherapists are men.

An even greater difficulty for my wife and myself, however, and the one which caused us to agree that I should work with a group alone, was our inability to "unwind" after everyone had gone home. There were some things that I needed to ventilate to her. There were some high and low experiences with concomitant emotions which she needed to share with me. The first thing we knew, we were talking, evaluating, and emoting into the wee hours of the morning. Sometimes there was hostility and anxiety, and neither of us was able to give consolation to the other. Often it was a rather short night, followed by a weary day. If we had been professional enough to have had a half-hour evaluation that night or the following day, turned it off by taking a walk or going out for a milkshake, we could have avoided this difficulty and strengthened our teamwork. We are smarter now and are leading various groups successfully as a team.

One Counselor or Cocounselors?

I am sure that for years to come there will be professional debates raging about the kind of leadership a group should have. Some will insist that a trained counselor or pastor who has worked individually with several couples and has formed them into a group in which he performs a uniform leadership role will provide the best kind of help. Others, especially in clinical settings and more particularly where cost of services is not a consideration, will effectively use and encourage two well-trained cotherapists, male and female whenever possible. Still others, both pastors and marriage counselors, will work together with their wives in a kind of team approach which makes up for its lack of professional training by providing the sort of natural marital dynamics, the husband and wife interrelationships and insights which cultivate healing communications.

Each approach could be carefully documented as an effective method. Chaplain Bruninga, working alone, has found his work so effective that he has expanded it to include group counseling in a community agency in addition to the hospital. Therefore a priest or pastor ought not to sidestep this form of ministry because he does not have a wife or woman cotherapist. Many pastors whose wives are unavailable or ineffective in this form of ministry can still be completely competent as enablers of group life.

The trained cotherapist style also has merit. Dr. Linden and his associates in Philadelphia consider two therapists as the significant choice. They prefer a man and a woman. They argue that dual therapists support one another in sharing stress. Two people can observe the action from different vantage points. A man-woman team serves as a model comparable to a good, communicating marriage. Husband and wife roles, male and female points of view are provided in the leadership team.[7] I do not have any evidence available showing ministers or priests working with trained women psychologists. But I see no reason why such a cooperative effort could not be successful when such persons are available, and particularly where the pastor is working through a community agency or in a highly structured church counseling program. Although there are examples of male chaplains and counselors working together, I do not know of two pastors leading a group. My own biases make this approach the least desirable of all methods. Busy pastors would not normally have the time to establish and maintain the kind of teamwork necessary for shared leadership. More important, probably, is the loss of the male-female leadership roles if two men are involved. There is a certain sense of fairness or balance when both a man and a woman are present. The deck is not stacked.

A pastor and his wife can lead a group together effectively. Some highly trained professional people will howl at the suggestion, but many of the sophisticated and somewhat artificial conditions which a clinical setting strives to achieve are actually inherent and normative in a husband and wife team. What the wife may lack in training, she may make up in humanness. Can she care? Can she listen? Can she open herself dialogically? Is her husband confident in her presence, and she in his? Does she know what it means to feel lonely at times or to be so angry with her husband that she could punch him in the nose? Can she put her arm around a weeping woman or say to the men, "You all just don't understand how a woman feels"—and then proceed to provide some insight into how a woman does feel?

Dr. Mace feels strongly that the pastor-wife leadership is the best style. He argues, in personal correspondence, that groups function best under dual leadership. He also is convinced that it is deeply meaningful for a pastor's wife to share with her husband a vital area of ministry in which they are truly equal partners.

The Reverend Marshall Stanton and his wife contracted together to perform this task as a joint ministry. They both took the Yokefellow tests and they shared insight slips. Pastor Stanton took the lead. His wife was supportive yet gave leadership of her own. They listened carefully to our mistakes. They tried to prepare themselves spiritually and emotionally before the meetings began. They had a baby-sitter for the children and held the group meeting in an informal room in the church. They set aside a half hour or so after the meeting to discuss what happened, made a few notations for the future, and then turned it off and went home.

Is This Work Church Business?

Should the pastor really get this deeply involved in human relationships? Many would say no, even shout no —and for a host of reasons. Abstract theology in both Catholic and Protestant circles has often kept both preacher and church from struggling with the disjoined human relationships which, like a slipped disc, result in anguish and pain.

> Many individuals already perceive the minister as a combination saint-dunce who is so engrossed with his sermons, prayer meetings, and other "holy" activities that he cannot even begin to understand the hard realities of life and suffering as experienced by ordinary mortals. . . . The counseling function . . . is an essential ingredient of the ministry. . . . The parishioner, seeing his minister blind to desperate human needs, may well question the existence of a meaningful relationship between the church and the day to day problems that confront him.[8]

Isn't it tragic the way we have divorced healing from the church! A person is supposed to go off somewhere and get well and then come back to "church." From time to time I receive a telephone call from some well-meaning soul in the church, giving me the name of such-and-such a family, and saying "They are such a nice couple and would make a lovely addition to our church." It was refreshing the other day for a rough layman to call me aside, mention a family, and say, "Preacher, you ought to go see 'em. They're in a hell of a fix, and the church ought to be able to help." The pastor is called upon not only to *care* for souls, but to *cure* souls.[9]

Some people in our churches will say that while it is all right for a minister to spend a little time counseling some troubled people, he really ought to spend the bulk of his time in more spiritual endeavors. I used to feel somewhat this way myself, particularly when my work was isolated, temporary, and crisis-oriented. Sometimes, even when I thought I had significantly helped people over a rough spot, I nevertheless felt that I had brought them no closer to God. Now, many within the Christian ministry will take severe issue with me here; they will say that the work of love is enough. Older liberal theologies would speak of service; newer humanistic theologies might talk of the Christ who is my needy neighbor. Yet, stimulating communications within a marriage or providing a channel for ventilating hostile feelings isn't enough. It is important to give bread to the hungry, but "man shall not live by bread alone" (Matt. 4:4). There *is* a difference between a secular counselor and a pastor. Two thoughts continually haunted me throughout our marriage counseling experiences. First, many times after a difficult counseling session, I would walk down the hall for a drink of water, thinking, "They are really lost souls. Their real problem is spiritual; they are selfish. They have been hating, hurting, cheating, lying, refusing to say 'I'm sorry,' and they wonder why things have gone sour." Biting my lip within the interview to avoid "God-talk," I nevertheless found myself clearly convinced that I was dealing with people who were alienated from the ways and will of God, but who were desperately hungry for him.

My second observation came by way of the group experiences themselves. Slowly people began to ask the right questions. Religious issues of purpose and meaning and hope began to come to the fore. To use a good old fashioned word, I would have to say that the most clear-cut "conversions" of my ministry occurred within the framework of the counseling groups. Sometimes the couples became so hungry for spiritual experience and truth that they sought out opportunities where confrontation and commitment were likely to take place. Many came to understand their insights within the group as actual spiritual encounters, the work of God in their lives.

> In the events of a counseling group, God may be known. In the process of group counseling, events happen which are of profound religious significance. Here one faces the *concrete shape of his own sin.* Here one makes *confession* and hears a word of forgiveness and acceptance. Here one learns to have *faith*—to trust his brethren and to trust himself. Such existential faith and trust is the ground upon which one may respond in trust to the living God. In counseling, *repentence* and *reconciliation* take place. One turns and becomes united to the "Thou" from whom he is separated. Here too, one learns to become *accountable* to another and to be *responsible* for others. In short, one learns to love another for his own sake. These are many of the "living facts" of the faith which many Christians believe but have experienced only in a limited way.

In addition, as one begins to re-experience, re-evaluate, and re-image himself and others, he discovers that he begins to *re-image his concept of God*. Whether in counseling or elsewhere, we are continually called upon to *break up the images graven in our minds* so that we may be grasped anew by the fullness of the reality of the living God. From the human side, hence, we maintain that group counseling as a method is consistent with the Biblical understanding of "the process of how we know God" and "the process of salvation."

This is not to say that group counseling alone is adequate. It is not. The other ministries of the church are necessary, such as the witness to the Word, the formal and informal expression of worship, and the fellowship and service within the Body of Christ. Group counseling, however, is a method which enables the church to become the church—the covenantal, confessional, caring people of God. It also becomes a place where laymen learn to engage in the prophetic and priestly ministry to each other as they hear confession, offer absolution in the name of Christ, and speak the truth in love.[10]

Interpreting to the Congregation

It is a wise pastor who, when entering the field of group work, and group counseling in particular, carefully interprets this action to his congregation. The counseling ministry requires a considerable amount of time, and that inevitably means a reshaping of the minister's time and task priorities. In one national study it was indicated that the average minister spends 2.2 hours per week in formal counseling. No one knows how much informal counseling he does. My own experience of the past few years reveals an expenditure of seven to twelve hours per week in individual and group counseling. Naturally some other important work didn't get done. In my case it was house to house

115

visitation which suffered. Because I had rather "drifted" into this emphasis, it was a year or so before I began to make a deliberate effort to identify my priorities to the congregation and seek to gain support for them. When some criticism began to appear, I then, rather belatedly, did some "time studies" for the administrative board. I also organized lay visitation for the shut-in and set aside some blocks of time during the summer and holidays for pastoral work. At first, I had a kind of false humility in keeping this counseling ministry rather quiet. I suppose I have resented those ministers who tend to brag about how much counseling they are doing. Sometimes I considered it a priestly matter, and therefore not really anybody's business. But when some congregational criticism began to surface, I hoisted the flag of my developing priorities. Frankly, that was all the people of the church wanted to know. In fact, they began to take a certain pride in the fact that their minister was thus engaged. Nearly everyone has a troubled marriage somewhere on his family tree, so there was considerable emotional support. "That's the kind of thing the church ought to be doing," some would say. One seventy-eight-year-old woman said, "I wish my husband and I could have been in a group like that forty years ago." Some good members even said, "Look pastor, don't bother to call on us unless we need you. We'd rather you would spend your time with families in trouble."

I'm sure that a pastor of a church needs to step back from time to time to see if everything is still in perspective. He is not a clinical person, and he dare not overlook the sick, the dying, the elderly. Nor can he let his leadership in worship and administration fall apart. So he must control this phase of his ministry, just as he must control and discipline the other areas of his work. The man who feeds his ego by overextending himself with troubled people and who, bleary-eyed, continually reports that he was up until 2:00 A.M. with a quarreling couple, ruins his effective ministry and his health just as surely as the man who runs from meeting to meeting or overemphasizes some other phase of the pastorate. But when the work is within a carefully disciplined structure and when the task is carefully explained, even "psychologically contracted" with the congregation, the pastor will have freedom, even encouragement to perform this variety of ministry. Then, too, there is the danger of moving from one congregation to another and presuming the kind of groundwork which was laid in the previous church. The whole interpretive task must be done all over again.

But the interpretation is exciting, both from the pulpit and with administrative groups. If group work is theologically valid as we are maintaining, then it has deep biblical and theological underpinnings. Sermons on group life, the New Testament church, spiritual and physical healings, marriage and the family—sermons which spring out of a deep caring for people—will be significantly appreciated by the congregation. The church may even begin to see the necessity for a greater depth of communal life within its fellowship. Furthermore, the interpretive work with administrative groups provides a dramatic framework on which to hang profound spiritual truths about what the church ought to be doing. Laymen may come to see themselves more clearly as a part of the mission of Christ in the world.

Toward a Greater Self-Confidence

Frankly, many men are discouraged with the pastoral ministry because they feel that nothing much is happening.

117

In the 1950s and early 60s, both Catholics and Protestants could see results in new buildings, enlarged budgets, and expanding memberships. But today, a man needs to see some results in the lives of people, or he will soon grow weary. Seward Hiltner, in *Profiles of the Ministry,* points out the difficulties of being a pastor today and reminds us of the many hats we must wear.[11] More severe evaluations are found in *A Church Without Priests.* At forty or forty-five years of age, one wants to be sure of his bearings. But many feel that they no longer know who they are. One priest said, "The balance sheet of my priestly life is a balance sheet of failure." [12] I have thought so often of that haunting line in the Beatles' song, Eleanor Rigby, which pictures Father McKinsey darning his socks, writing his sermon, conducting the funeral, but "no one was saved." One wag has said, "What can a minister do nowadays *without* hell and *with* the pill?" Well, hell has not disappeared, not from the bedrooms and kitchens of our land, and no pill is able to take away the loneliness and heartbreak of a twisted marriage. But the minister who watches a family kneeling at the communion rail who, a few months before were fighting in an attorney's office, does not find his balance sheet empty.

Prayer

The pastor has powers of healing open to him which are not open to anyone else. That is not to say that the clergyman has a monopoly on the work of the Holy Spirit. Far from it. Wherever there is healing, there is God; and the reality of God's healing is as certain in the operating room or on the psychiatrist's couch as it is in the pastor's study. Still, the minister and priest have some special spiritual assets. Prayer is a good example. It is often difficult for a clinical man to use any form of prayer within a group or to suggest it for individuals. He may be a man with a deep life of prayer himself. He may bow his head or get on his knees after someone has left his office, but in our society it would generally be considered unprofessional for him to use any form of prayer in his treatment. There are extremes of course. No one is turned on by the pious professional pray-er. On the other hand, some ministers and priests have been so turned off by religiosity that they bend over backward to avoid any form of prayer experience at all. But if these extremes are avoided, the pastor has a unique and rewarding opportunity to incorporate honest, natural prayer into the life of his group experience. What other professional man has the freedom to gather a group together at the close of a session, clasp hands, and simply recognize the awesome wonder of God's love? Many a counselor would envy the pastor's privilege of letting people silently or in child-like sentence prayers thank God for the insights and encouragements, the acceptance and self-affirmations which have been experienced. Often our time of prayer is simply a reminder that God has been in our midst all evening long, and we are stopping to recognize that fact and to thank him by name. Prayer must be honest, positive, supportive. In no way must a person be embarrassed, coerced, or offended. But we have had persons who didn't admit that they believed in God who were willing to participate in this closing ritual and on occasion, during sentence prayers say, "I'm glad that I can be myself with these people."

A few weeks ago a group with whom we had worked a year before invited my wife and me to go out to supper. Because we were moving, it would be our last chance to be together. As we were eating, one of the women, a Catholic, said, "Before we leave, we want to have our prayer circle." At the close of the meal, however, we were all talking, and we forgot. As they were paying the bill at the door, one of the men said, "We forgot our prayer circle." It was late and not many people were in the restaurant, but I'm sure that the one or two observers were surprised to see twelve people take hands and pray the Lord's prayer together as comfortably as if we had been in our own living room.

In addition to our group prayer experiences, we asked each person to have some meditative time each day and to pray, by name, for every individual in the group. Again and again, couples expressed gratitude that others were praying for them daily.

My personal convictions that a pastor has opportunities and resources not usually available to the clinician were strongly reinforced by Hiltner and Colston. They state that "people seeking counseling help from a pastor when other conditions are approximately equal, will tend to progress slightly farther and faster in the same amount of time than they will in another setting." [13] Knowles goes further and says, "In a church where members engage in depth dialogue with each other, the word 'slightly' can be changed to 'significantly.' Five of the seven counseling groups at the Church of the Savior in Washington, D.C., moved to a level in one month that would have taken six months for groups in a nonchurch setting to achieve." [14]

This statement also points to an additional asset of the minister. He has a wider fellowship of concerned people beyond the counseling group. He has a place in which people can continue to grow after the therapy is over. While it is true that the church is only an option, it becomes an ever increasingly live option for the couples. Having experienced a level of communal participation which they had not known before, they are often the first ones to attend a spiritual life retreat, join a sharing group, or help form a worship workshop. What a powerful back-up resource the pastor has to be able to offer a dialogical, caring fellowship to provide an environment for ongoing growth and personal and family support! If the local congregation isn't that open and that concerned, some changes had better be made, and the couples in the group will help to make them.

Laws

A brief word would be appropriate to consider current and forthcoming legislation in the field of counseling. There is a strong effort among psychologists and counselors to make marriage counseling increasingly professional. The American Association of Marriage Counselors celebrated its twenty-fifth anniversary in 1967, and throughout its history has been working for standards of certification and legal restrictions. To date, several states have passed laws pertaining to the certification or licensing of marriage counselors. Laws have also been demanded by the general public because of unscrupulous practitioners, outright frauds, and other irregularities of counseling. Charles H. Dickinson, in evaluating marriage counselor laws, believes that additional laws should be passed and that they should be increasingly restrictive. In California, for example, legislation does not apply to ministers, priests, rabbis, or those licensed to practice law or medicine, or to any organization which is both nonprofit and charitable. Dickinson argues that these exemptions are weakening to the standards of the profession.

Part of the problem is that there is little legal definition as to what a minister is in the first place. In addition, "self-ordained or disillusioned ministers who have either given up their churches, or, who have been expelled, have, in some instances apparently turned to marriage counseling as a livelihood." [15]

At this point, there is no legislation which restricts bona fide clergymen from performing counseling services. The issue in the future will probably hinge on the concept of advertising. Most clergymen are not interested in advertising in any billboard sense, yet some might very well like to make their services known through family service centers, telephone listings, etc. Churches ought to watch this development quite carefully because, on one hand, we should be as eager as the professional counselors and psychologists to eliminate quacks and charlatans and, on the other hand, we want to maintain the legitimacy of pastors to work with troubled people. Undoubtedly the answer lies in the area of maintaining professional integrity and working within the framework of the church or a community service organization.

An increasing number of clergymen will undoubtedly be receiving special training through the Clinical Pastoral Education program (C.P.E.) and through graduate degrees in psychology. Some will receive various forms of accreditation including membership in professional organizations. Some, in clinical settings or on the staff of large churches, will devote full time to counseling, and these persons will probably be more highly trained than most professional secular counselors. But for the average pastor serving in a local congregation, the opportunities for service in the field of marriage counseling seem to be practically unlimited for the foreseeable future.

Those who would argue that we should have a large corps of counseling specialists totally apart from the pastoral ministry miss the mark on several counts. First, according to some experts, the approximately 235,000 parish clergymen are seeing approximately 6,570,000 troubled persons each year. It would require approximately 65,000 specialists to replace the counseling done by these parish ministers. At the present time, the membership of the American Association of Marriage and Family Counselors numbers about 2,000.

But much more important is the theological consideration. The specialist is not a pastor; counseling of this nature ought to grow out of a pastoral theology. No one should know better than the parish minister the harsh reality of human suffering among millions of individuals and the possibility that the normal combination of humility, wisdom, and compassion in many thousands of ministers is a potent weapon against suffering.

Training Possibilities

How can a person prepare himself to work with marriage counseling groups? On one hand we have pointed to the necessary human qualities, the pastoral involvement, and the need simply to get started. On the other hand we have referred to many sophisticated clinical writers. Formal training does not necessarily make a good counselor. Yet, certain types of learning in seminaries and hospitals can be extremely productive.

Increasingly, group experiences, often with the wives included, are becoming the norm in seminaries and in medical schools. One seminary has small cluster groups of couples for sharing, support, and supervision all the way through theological training. This year at Menninger's, physicians who are in psychiatric residency have been formed into small experimental groups with their wives in order to be supportive, but also to test and observe group life. An increasing number of ministers are taking various amounts of clinical training, and there is inevitably an emphasis on group process as the participants work together. In fact, the Association for Clinical Pastoral Education, with headquarters at 475 Riverside Drive, New York, has standardized requirements which include two forms of small group experience. There is always a group that stresses peer relationships. Also, a participant is inevitably in a supervisory group relationship. Many skills are learned; a person is sensitized (made perceptive of feelings), he gains experience in contracting mutual expectations, and he learns how to set personal and group goals. He participates in periodic evaluations. General hospitals and mental health centers across the country are providing C.P.E. training for ministers and priests. Course schedules can be one day a week, ten weeks in the summer, or a full year of residency.

Workshops and short-term training experiences are popping up. Pastors who are already counseling individuals will profit from psychodrama workshops, encounter training, or group marriage counseling seminars. Transactional analysis is becoming increasingly popular as a counseling stance. Information may be obtained from the Department of Pastoral Services, Bi-State Mental Health Foundation, Ponca City, Oklahoma. Chaplain Bruce Zellmer provides intensive short-term T.A. training as well as C.P.E. supervision.

Reuel Howe, at his Institute for Advanced Pastoral Studies near Detroit, leads personal growth and professional development seminars for pastors and wives. These seminars generally last six days. While they are not designed to teach counseling skills, they nonetheless provide growth in human and marital relationships, improvement in communication skills, and experience in small group process.

As has been indicated several times, the Yokefellow plan has been the foundation on which our experimentation was built. Although the Yokefellow Prayer Therapy Groups were not specifically designed for married couples, the program is highly adaptable to this approach. In fact, new tests have just been developed to be used in couples' groups. The organization, which has been encouraged by Dr. Elton Trueblood, has been most famous for its small group rehabilitation work in prisons. Today, however, there are thousands of Yokefellow groups all across the country, and they range in leadership from mature laymen to highly professional persons. In terms of group composition, they vary from people wanting personal and spiritual growth to those individuals who are deeply disturbed. Regular leadership training conferences are held, generally in Burlingame, California. Dr. Cecil G. Osborne is the very capable executive director. It is possible to begin a group program by carefully reading *Prayer Can Change Your Life*. The complete Yokefellow information packet includes material on how to lead a Yokefellow group and is available from Yokefellow, Inc., 209 Park Road, Burlingame, California 94010.

Because so little has been prepared for clergyman in the area of marriage groups per se, I have recorded a series of cassettes in cooperation with the Family Enrichment Bureau and Tidings under the theme "The Pastor and Marriage Therapy Groups." The six tapes run in length about twenty minutes each, and they may be used by an individual minister or, perhaps more profitably, by a very small group of clergymen who would then spend some time discussing the material. The titles of the six tapes are: "Pastors and Effective Marriage Counseling," "What Is a Marriage Therapy Group," "How Do You Get Going: The First Meeting," "Group Process," "The Pastor As Leader: Competence and Confidence," and "Resources and Results." [16] It is hoped that this material will enable an experienced and well trained pastor to have the confidence and resources so that he will move into this form of group work. I have also written a book called *Tell Me Again, I'm Listening.*[17] It is designed primarily for marriage enrichment, but it could be used in counseling either as "springboard" material or for auxiliary reading.

The perceptive reader will note that each training experience requires some "translation" on the part of the minister or priest before applying it to marriage groups. The field is so new that the ground is still being broken. Marriage counseling skills need to be adapted to a group setting. Group skills have to be reoriented to a couples environment. Almost all group therapy material is developed for random individuals, but it can be appropriated for marriage use. Allusion has already been made to efforts to include observers in existing groups. Though difficult, it can be done by careful negotiation with the group. Most group therapists and most group counselors over the past few years simply began on their own. Fortified with all the skills that can be mustered, I expect that the same thing must happen in the field of marriage group work.

In many parts of the country, methods of consultation and supervision can be devised by imaginative pastors. Key professional people who can help bridge the gap between the counseling world and the parish are chaplains in hospitals, counselors in Catholic or Lutheran Social Services, and psychologists in mental health centers. Many agencies consider assistance for the clergy as a prime responsibility and offer consultation without fee. For example, the Department of Pastoral Services at Bi-State Mental Health will help a pastor set up a plan of action, allow him to bring in tapes that show what is happening in his group, and encourage occasional long distance calls or personal visits to evaluate progress. Professional laymen in many parishes will gladly assist their pastor in his efforts to begin this ministry. They will also often do consultations on a perplexing case. Some denominations are setting aside funds for consultations of this type. So much marriage work needs to be done—most agencies have waiting lists—that I know of no one who is jealous about his own clientele. For every professional person who discourages a pastor from treading in such deep water, there will be an equally qualified professional who will urge him to dive in and will offer to lend a helping hand.

Chapter VI
The Church in Search of Renewal

In England a woman named Florence Allshorn began a missionary renewal center. Miss Allshorn noticed that zealous young missionaries often became discouraged in their first tour of duty. So she created a community of healing and restoration for such missionaries. She wrote:

> In the past the emphasis for those trying to live a more dedicated Christian life had been on the need for an unusual effort to alter situations single-handed. Now the leading of the Spirit seemed to be that the witness of *living together* a truly Christian life was more needed than solitary greatness.[1]

A Lost Sense of Koinonia

Something like this experience seems to be happening to the church today. Not only are we groping for a *theology* of the church, but we are searching for an *experience* of the church. The converts after Pentecost "devoted themselves to the apostles' teaching and fellowship, to the breaking of bread and the prayers" (Acts 2:42). The church

128

has never had as many well-instructed preachers and teachers as today. There is scarcely a place in the world where it is impossible to receive the Holy Communion. Undoubtedly prayers are being offered in churches and in private closets. But in our church life we are starved for *koinonia,* the New Testament word for fellowship. We hunger for that intimate experience of togetherness which characterized the New Testament church. Our existing church organizations are often squeezed dry of deep interpersonal relationships. Many of our best people never get through the work of the church into its spiritual life and mission. Robert Raines quotes a personal conversation with a German theologian: "Today (unlike the time of the Reformation) the problem is not how to find a gracious God, but how to find a gracious neighbor." [2]

Recently I visited one of the living room groups of our church women's organization. Because there were only about a dozen women who met regularly in one another's homes, I assumed that group process would be significant. I thought they would be a kind of "family" in Christ. They had invited me to give the program. Instead I simply asked them to go around the circle and tell some important spiritual experience in their lives. I could scarcely believe what happened. One woman said that her son had recently left for the war in Vietnam and that she was praying for him each day. But what surprised me, in fact terrified me, was that no one in the room knew about it. Here was a lonely mother supposedly amid Christian friends, but they were totally oblivious of her deepest fears. Tears came to another woman's eyes as she told about the child they had lost some years before and how God's love had carried her through the darkness. Again, no one in the group even knew she had ever lost that child. And so it went. The ladies had spent their time month after month talking about whether to have ham and green beans or meat loaf and corn at the church suppers. They didn't know one another at all. No life-giving *koinonia* existed. A new convert or a seeker would not have discovered a caring community in their homes. No wonder Sam Shoemaker once said, "Putting an eager seeker after Christ into the conventional church is like putting a live chicken under a dead hen."

Some of our couples tried to enter other groups within the church. Often they became discouraged. Everything was so superficial, so rigid, so unconcerned, and so impersonal. These struggling souls were fighting battles of heaven and hell, life and death. They could scarcely tolerate chit-chat.

> We are simply not prepared to handle radical doubt or commitment. Somebody becomes fired with real concern but after an evening or two at the Men's Club or the Couples' Club or the Women's Group is overwhelmed with disillusionment. Here is the major problem. Our conventional structure is not geared to enable people to come into deep personal relationship.[3]

During the past two years my wife and I have been meeting with a small group (six couples) of ministers and their wives for an afternoon and evening once every two months. The men finished seminary about three years ago. It was part of a pilot project of The United Methodist Church and the National Council of Churches to aid young pastors in professional growth. We quickly discovered that they were not asking questions about preaching or church administration. They were too lonely, too depressed, too hungry for Christian friends to take another course in church history or theology. They were frustrated and anxious. They had been trained in urban seminaries and felt alienated from rural laymen. They distrusted other clergymen. Ecclesiastical authorities appeared to them to be remote and aloof. Communication with them was thin and strained. Deep-seated hurts from childhood were still eating at vital emotions. Some were thinking about leaving the ministry; others were questioning their marriages.

We dropped the whole professional agenda. We spent our time sharing where we were in terms of our immediate needs. We ate together, usually at a restaurant, in a happy fellowship supper. We had a prayer circle together, although as "professionals" we were more hesitant, more afraid of being phony than laymen would be. Nevertheless, good things began to happen. We talked openly. We shared fears and hurts. We prayed for each other at home. Two of the couples gained the courage to seek counseling. Our fellowship, even though only occasional, became so significant to each of us that we went to great lengths to maintain it. We live all over the state, but, for each meeting, nearly everyone was present. Some drove over three hundred miles each way in order to attend. My wife and I were supposed to be advisors for the group but we quickly found that the group was an indispensible means of support for us as well as for the others.

As I observe the various youth movements which focus around the name and teachings of Jesus, I note that they inevitably have one thing in common. They experience *koinonia*. The Jesus Freaks, the young pentecostals, the youth who are a part of "The Way" and those countless communals of varying forms, all are inevitably involved in human encounter. One of the boys (age sixteen) in my congregation who was highly suicidal and depressed, recently was released by a private psychiatric center. He became a part of a "Jesus" group. With his doctor's permission, he stopped taking his medications. Each night he assembles with other young people for study of the Scriptures. Each day, in cooperation with others, he sells flowers and gives a witness. Each person has a "shepherd"—another young person who looks after him while he is new in the movement. In the fellowship they tell of their troubles, their trials, and their victories.

Remnants of real brotherhood days are still in the vocabulary of our organized churches. Some old fashioned Methodists or Baptists still call their ministers "Brother." Some Catholic orders use the term "Brother" for certain classifications. But many youth are looking for a family relationship deeper than ecclesiology, one that is open and human. Raines, in thinking of church renewal, wrote:

> The church is the family of Christ. Jesus spoke of his disciples as brothers and sisters (Mark 3:35), called them to an allegiance higher than blood-tie loyalty (Luke 14: 26), and promised them new brothers and sisters in the fellowship of His followers (Mark 10:30). There are three constitutive elements that characterize our participation in the family of Christ. First, we belong to Christ in belonging to each other. Second, we learn Christ's love by learning to love each other. Third, the family of Christ is a ministering community.[4]

The New Testament Experience: <u>Koinonia</u>

Depth studies of the word *koinonia,* are interesting and deserve our attention.

> Koinonia is derived from the root "koin"—"common" and means accordingly "one who has something in common with someone else." It should be kept in mind, how-

ever, that sometimes the thing which is in common is really a person or persons. . . . The primary idea expressed by koinonia and its cognates is not that of association with another person or other persons, but that of participation in something in which others also participate.[5]

Demosthenes used this expression, "they will share the consequences along with everyone else." Plato in *The Republic* referred to "the participation by the women" in a common activity. Again, speaking of a community of wives, i.e., wives held and shared in common, Plato used the expression, "the participation in the women."

In the Septuagint, reference is made to the "sharing of life in marriage." For the most part, however, the word is not too important in Old Testament thinking, for the Scriptural emphasis is on Israel as a total people, a covenant people. The commonality is in being the children of Abraham, Isaac, and Jacob, a people led by the hand out of bondage, a nation chastised by the rod of Assyria and yet reclaimed, even as Hosea reclaimed Gomer. In the New Testament church, however, the word took on unusual significance and special meaning. The early Christians were not a political entity. They were scattered groups of people who shared common experiences and beliefs. Often they lived amid a hostile environment. They shared much in common, including, at times, their property (Acts 2:44).

They were sympathetic with one another and shared each others sufferings. The Corinthians shared in the sufferings of Paul (II Cor. 1:7). The Philippians shared in Paul's sufferings in the sense that they had a lively and active sympathy with him (Phil. 4:14). In Hebrews, companionship even included the sharing of reproach.

The word "participation" often correctly translates *koin-*

onia. There is participation in the Holy Spirit (II Cor. 13:15 and Phil. 2:1-3). *Koinonia* can mean both a divine and a human participation. Blaine B. Rader in an article, "Koinonia and the Therapeutic Relationship," writes

> Koinonia refers to a mystical sharing between men and God. . . . In addition, there is a simultaneous horizontal sharing which is described as "koinonia.". . . This relationship of those in Christian community is marked by love, unity, mutual sympathy and service.[6]

This mingling of the "vertical" and the "horizonal" is most clearly seen in the experience of Holy Communion. The bread which we break, is it not a participation in the body of Christ? The wine which we drink, is it not a participation in the blood of Christ (I Cor. 10:16)? *Koinonia* describes an experience of very specific intimate sharing. In our group life, midway in the evening, two or three people would get up and serve a cup of coffee and a cookie to each person. It was more than a break; it was a symbolic act of sharing, a "breaking of bread together" in an atmosphere of unity and love. Think how much *more* power was generated in those early Christian communities when they actually broke the loaf as a participation in Jesus and his Way. When they drank of the cup, it was a total involvement of their lives together. It bound them to the ministry and passion of the Lord; it charactrized their oneness as a community of love and trust. "Because there is one loaf, we who are many are one body, for we all partake of the same loaf" (I Cor. 10:17).

Robert Spike in *Tests of a Living Church* wrote:

> Koinonia was a recognizable togetherness that people felt in their whole being, their mind and body. This to-

getherness was there only because they felt the reality of God impinging upon their minds and physical beings.[7]

Healing in Koinonia

That continual healing took place within the fellowship of the early Christians there can be little doubt. The dramatic examples of healing by the apostles were not isolated individual acts, but were part and parcel of Christian community life. The Christians were continually together. They were honest with one another. They prayed for one another. They were "filled with the Spirit." No wonder a power in their midst influenced their bodies and their minds.

A negative, but vivid example is found in the experience of Ananias and his wife Sapphira. The Scriptures record that this couple sold their farm, but hid half of the money and brought the other half to the fellowship. This example has been often used by preachers in terms of stewardship and financial contributions. But the real point is in terms of *koinonia*. Bruce Larson is absolutely correct when he interprets the matter thus:

> Two very fine people, Ananias and Sappira, dropped dead in the Church (Acts, chapter five). They weren't drunks. As far as we know, he wasn't cheating on her. They went to prayer meetings. They were more than tithers. *But they were pretending something that wasn't true before God and before His people.* Death is inevitable, whether physical, mental, psychic, or spiritual. Ananias and Sappira were *pretenders.*[8]

Lies, dishonesty, masking, hiddenness—these are anathema to *koinonia*. Peter, in order to maintain the total honesty of the community ripped off their masks. Peoples' lives were literally at stake. If bodies were to be healed, if minds were to be restored to sanity, if souls were to be cleansed, then deception had to be purged. Continual openness had to be maintained or the power would be lost.

The letter of James provides a positive description of *koinonia* in the New Testament church. The words of Jesus are quoted to help assure total honesty within the fellowship. "But above all my brethren, do not swear, either by heaven or earth or any other oath, but let your yes be yes and your no be no, that you may not fall under condemnation" (5:12). This phrase has often been entangled in sophistry of all sorts, including legalistic arguments about taking oaths in court. The full weight of it, however, comes down on the dreadful necessity of being totally honest. Think how many months it sometimes takes in a marriage group before some persons will trust the group enough to share their fears and guilts! Every member of the group is keenly aware that healing is taking place when someone begins honestly to share his thoughts and feelings as they really are. In our evaluations, we asked each person to signify who in the group had not been helped. Almost invariably there would be a comment like, "So and so wasn't helped because he wouldn't open up." In the early church, every participant was expected to "tell it like it is."

Prayer

James wants the everyday stresses of life to be dealt with in and by the church. "Is any one among you suffering? Let him pray" (5:13). This can sound like rejection or seclusion. Some think it means to go off by yourself and pray. Not at all. The key idea is the fellowship. The words really mean If anyone is suffering, let him be a part of the prayers of the church. Let him be a part of the prayer life of the people, supported by their prayers, and praying himself openly to God for release.

James stresses the efficacy of communal prayer for the sick and for the sin-sick.

> Is any among you sick? Let him call for the elders of the church, and let them pray over him, anointing him with oil in the name of the Lord; and the prayer of faith will save the sick man, and the Lord will raise him up; and if he has committed sins, he will be forgiven(5:14-15).

Again James admonishes the community to pray for one another (5:16). In our groups we discovered that people were pulling for one another. Unbelievable power is unleashed when people know that someone is praying for them each day.

Confession

The church has always suspected that it was in the business of lifting guilt. In the early church there was open sharing of hurts and guilts right in the fellowship. "Confess your sins to one another . . . that you may be healed." (James 5:16) The familiar passage from 1 John, so often used to give assurance in a worship service, actually referred to open confession within the *koinonia*.

> If we say [in the fellowship] we have no sin, we deceive ourselves, and the truth is not in us. If we confess our sins [to the community], he is faithful and just, and will forgive our sins and cleanse us from all unrighteousness (I John 1:8-9).

Both Catholics and Protestants have lost the experience of New Testament confession. In Protestantism, we have preached forgiveness, but it has often been a form of cheap grace. In Catholicism, the priestly confessional has become so formalized and sacradotal that little real healing occurs. For five centuries there was no other form of confession among Christians except open confession for both public and private sins. All sins were to be confessed so that the sacrifice, the offering of themselves in the Holy Communion, might be pure. As late as the fifth century, Pope Leo the Great in a letter to a bishop, said it was "sufficient that confessions be made to the priests in secret." Even this instruction did not forbid public confession. It was not until the thirteenth century that the structure became so restrictive that confession was only to be made to ordained priests.[9]

Unfortunately, Protestants threw the baby out with the bath. Both Calvin and Luther wanted to maintain the value of private confession to a pastor on a voluntary basis. It was the abuse of the confessional, not the confession itself, which troubled Luther. Luther wrote:

> Private confession . . . is wholly commendable, useful and indeed necessary. I would not have it cease, but rather I rejoice that it exists in the Church of Christ, for it is the one and only remedy for troubled consciences.[10]

Calvin's emphasis was much the same. In the Institutes he urged that the confession (1) be made to God (even though in man's presence); (2) that it be voluntary; (3) that it be regarded as nonsacramental; (4) that it be made to man after being made to God; (5) that it rest on prior satisfaction made by God in Jesus Christ.

> Therefore let every believer remember that it is his duty, if he feels such secret anguish or affiliction from a

sense of his sins, that he cannot extricate himself without some exterior aid, not to neglect the remedy offered him by the Lord; which is, that in order to alleviate his distress, he should use private confession with his pastor, and, to obtain consolation, should privately implore his assistance, whose office is, both publicly and privately, to comfort the people of God with the doctrine of the Gospel.[11]

While these ideas of the reformers lacked the power of confession before the whole church, they nevertheless maintained a psychological awareness of one man's need to tell another. What a tragedy that Protestantism diminished even this simple pastoral assistance to the guilt-ridden! Often we lost the human relationship entirely. Dr. Mowrer is adamant on this point.

> Even the *one* "human intermediary" was eliminated, and the faithful were admonished to take their sins "directly to God in prayer." This strategy neatly neutralized the mercenary abuse of confession (including the sale of indulgences and bogus religious relics); but, as we now are realizing, four and a half centuries later, *it has also left us with no fully satisfactory means of dealing with personal guilt.* Today's Christianity has almost completely discarded the very tools that made it a world force and a redemptive therapeutic power such as had not been known before and has not been known since.[12]

Guilt is one of the great tragedies of the human predicament, and the Christian faith and community are meant to deal with it. The husband who lies about money feels guilt. The wife who cheats in sex experiences shame. They need a way to be made whole again. Carl Jung understands it psychologically in this way:

> There appears to be a conscience in mankind which severely punishes the man who does not somehow and at

some time, at whatever cost to his pride, cease to defend and assert himself, and instead confess himself fallible and human. . . . No way of escape from guilt is open to the sufferer except through a functioning confession.[13]

Oscar Wilde, out of the anguish of his heart, put it so picturesquely. "A man's very highest moment is, I have no doubt, when he kneels in the dust and beats his breast, and tells all the sins of his life." [14]

Our religious cure for guilt has become so weak because we have diluted our medicine. If we were truthful with one another we would feel clean. The idea of the priesthood of all believers means that others can be priests for me as well as meaning that I can be a priest for myself. If a man is really to be free, he must make amends wherever possible. That is precisely what Jesus had in mind when he said,

So if you are offering your gift at the altar, and there remember that your brother has something against you, leave your gift there before the altar and go; first be reconciled to your brother, and then come and offer your gift (Matt. 5:23-24).

Whenever the church has been most alive, most vibrant with the renewing work of the Holy Spirit, the dialogical relationships which included communal confession were practiced. That truth was not only evidenced in the early church, but it was true among many of the Anabaptists, the Wesleyan class meetings, among Pentecostals, and in certain religious communities. St. Basil was the first to make the ascetic practice of confession of sin an integral part of the monastic discipline. In the fourth century, St. Basil insisted that every monk he ordained must confess his faults either to one or more members of the community. He took the admonition of St. James to "confess your faults one to another" seriously. He said to his brotherhood:

> Every subject, if he intends to make any progress worth mentioning and to be confirmed in a mode of life that accords with the precepts of our Lord Jesus Christ, ought not to conceal within himself any movement of his soul, not yet utter any thoughtless word, but he should reveal the secrets of his heart to those of his brethren whose office it is to exercise a compassionate and sympathetic solicitude for the weak.[15]

His emphasis on auricular confession influenced all of Christendom. The deliberate revealing of the secrets of the heart to one another, as Basil put it, contributed to an incalculable degree to the development of the spiritual life of the whole community. He wrote in his rules, "For vice kept secret is a festering wound in the soul."

In our own time, the Protestant community at Taizé, France, regards the confession to be of such value that they practice it without fail. Some of their rules read as follows:

> Do not fear to share the trials of others, nor be afraid of suffering. For it is often at the bottom of the abyss that the perfection of joy is given in communion with Jesus Christ. Perfect joy gives itself. Acknowledge your mistakes with simplicity (*reconnais simplement tes faux-pas*), in the transparency of brotherly love without finding therein a pretext for discerning those of others. Wherever they are, the Brothers practice brief and frequent sharing with one another. Simplicity is found in the free joy of a Brother who forsakes the obsession of his own progress or backslidings, in order to fix his gaze on the light of Christ.[16]

Dietrich Bonhoeffer is best known for his private meditations and writings while in prison, but his leadership at the seminary where he taught was highly communal in nature, and included a kind of open confession. Bonhoeffer made it known that the communion celebration required mutual reconciliation, and without liturgical procedure, he urged the ordinands to confess privately to one of the brethren before the time of communion. At first there was some embarrassed resentment. No one was ever quite sure how many confessions were made, but as the communal experience became a monthly event, there "was an indefinable feeling that things had changed." One day Bonhoeffer himself asked one of the young men—one who was quite inexperienced in such matters—to hear his confession.

Bonhoeffer wrote:

> My dear brethren, anyone who has ever had the experience of being wrested away from grave sin by God and the receiving forgiveness, anyone to whom God in such an hour has sent a brother to whom he can tell his sin, anyone who knows the resistance put up by his sin to that help because he does not really want to be helped, and has nevertheless found himself absolved from his sin by his brother in the name and at the behest of God—will lose all desire to judge and to apportion blame. All he will ask is a share in his brother's burden, and to serve, to help, to forgive, without measure without conditions, without end.[17]

Mission

It has been a long time since people in our respectable middle class churches talked seriously about "lost" people. In theological circles, hell might be discussed intellectually, but it is difficult to find people trembling over the personal prospect of eternal damnation. It's true that sometimes we sing some old missionary songs which indicate that there are lost people in some heathen land who are going to hell because they do not know of Christ, but these songs have become increasingly distasteful. It is usually when a missionary has just returned from Africa or Asia that we sing this hymn:

> Behold how many thousands still are lying,
> Bound in the darksome prison-house of sin,
> With none to tell them of the Savior's dying,
> Or of the life He died for them to win.
> Publish Glad tidings; Tidings of peace;
> Tidings of Jesus, Redemption and release.[18]

But the tragedy is that there are people next door who are living lives of quiet desperation. People weren't speaking eschatologically when they referred to their marriages as living hell. The mission field today is everywhere—wherever there are sick, lonely, troubled souls. And their name is legion. Dag Hammerskjold understood loneliness. He wrote: "The anguish of loneliness brings blasts from the storm center of death." [19]

A few days ago I visited a beautiful new church structure in a Western Kansas town. The building was just consecrated a few months ago. It cost a quarter of a million dollars. As I walked out of the church, I noticed an unusually lovely home directly across the street. When I commented about it to the pastor, he replied that the lady who lived there had just committed suicide. Her husband had died, she had no children, and she kept mostly to herself. One night she went into her closed garage, started the motor, and surrounded herself with carbon monoxide. A neighbor noticed a light on in the garage, thought it unusual and strange, but decided against looking into the situation.

That little beacon of light sent out a feeble cry for help, but no aid came.

What a parable of the church in America today. In our beautiful sanctuaries we talk about mission while people die across the street. Highly educated men preach sermons on family life while marriages inside and outside the congregation rot and disintegrate. Many social problems—crime, drugs, mental illness—can be traced directly to sick family life. The homes of America—what a mission field!

From a moralistic point of view we are talking about sinners—people who commit adultery, who are in and out of divorce courts, who drink too much at the country club or the neighborhood tavern, who grit their teeth and seethe with selfishness and resentment. These are precisely the people that the "body of Jesus," the church, needs to touch —with a touch that heals, that restores, that saves. Jesus was criticized as being a friend of sinners.

> And as he sat at table in the house, behold many tax collectors and sinners came and sat down with Jesus and his disciples. And when the Pharisees saw this, they said to his disciples, "Why does your teacher eat with tax collectors and sinners?" But when he heard it, he said, "Those who are well have no need of a physician, but those who are sick. Go and learn what this means, 'I desire mercy and not sacrifice.' For I came not to call the righteous, but sinners" (Matt. 9:10-13).

Tracey K. Jones, Jr., writes:

> Always the mission field is where people talk to each other about human existence. . . . Today the separation of faith and unbelief is more like a no-man's land, a zone of silence, than it is a "lost" village waiting for the missionary to come across the mounatins.[20]

Many of us are looking for a "handle," a specific way of relating the Gospel to the human condition. We use words like "involvement," but we are not very deeply involved in human hurt. We talk about "relevancy," but most people outside the church do not see us as particularly relevant. But the couples who were incorporated into marriage group counseling had no such indifference. They were fighting the battles of life and death. When the church cared enough to reach out to them, they felt it was the reaching hand of Christ himself.

Insights for Other Healing Groups

The concepts of this approach to treatment-growth have far wider possibilities than just with troubled marriages. The church in mission can use the same precepts in other forms. For example, our church organized a small group of younger divorced and widowed women who called themselves the "Coterie" group. Their purpose: to encourage and support one another in a sharing dialogue, study, fellowship, and prayer. So often divorcées feel cut off from the church. This group became one of the most active centers of Christian fellowship within the congregation. Several began teaching in the church school, taking part in the women's work, and attending special services. Women who are trying to work, raise children, and take care of financial and property matters all by themselves need all the support they can get. What better way is there for them to receive that support than to come together in their mutual need and share? I did not meet with the group often enough, nor did I structure it in such a way that it could be called a counseling group. But there were enough personal problems and enough vital expressions of group process that such a direction could have been possible. In any event, it was valuable Christian fellowship.

From time to time, every pastor has a teen-ager come in to his study who is confused, sullen, and in some kind of trouble. Usually he or she is doing poorly in school and is at odds with his parents. Psychologists in clinical settings are experimenting with group process with such teenagers and they are having creative and exciting results. Some expand the process to work with the whole family. A group for distressed teen-agers would be an exciting adventure.

Many ministers are transforming their youth program into teen-age covenant groups. My sons, who are seventeen and fifteen-years old, are finding their most meaningful form of Christian experience in a weekly "Covenant" group of seven or eight teenagers who meet with a mature Christian layman. The Fellowship of Christian Athletes has built its program not only on the great rallies but also on the weekly "huddle" group which meets in the homes or schools. What an infinite number of possibilities lie open in *koinonia* with young people. They range all the way from therapy to simple support groups. The imaginative pastor, working in the framework of a dialogical church, has a mission field "white unto the harvest" right in his own parish.

Evangelism

In this total discussion, we have not used the word "grace" very often, although it has been implicit in countless comments. But if there is to be renewal in the church and a radical new involvement with people in their spiritual sickness, then there must be a new appreciation and experience of grace as we understand it in the scriptures. Old moralisms must be vigorously discarded; fresh appreciation for the unfathomable love of God must be engendered. To be a therapeutic community, we necessarily need to see the world through the eyes of the Savior of men, who came not to condemn, but to save.

> Moralistic pietism views the church as a converted community surrounded by an evil world. . . . If the church is defined in this way, its task becomes that of getting as many of the good people into its organization as possible, and separating itself as much as possible from the world hastening toward corruption. . . . Victorian morality became undissolubly wedded with an introverted, subjectively oriented religious pietism so as to produce a curious picture of the church as a community consisting not of sinners whom God has pardoned but of the morally strait-laced who rejoice in their own righteousness. This is a far cry from the way the early church understood itself.[21]

The Letter to the Ephesians tells of a grace which accepts the unworthy.

> He destined us in love to be his sons through Jesus Christ, according to the purposes of his will, to the praise of his glorious grace which he freely bestowed on us in the Beloved. . . . For by grace you have been saved through faith, and this is not your own doing, it is the gift of God. . . . In him we have redemption through his blood, the forgiveness of our trespasses, according to the riches of his grace which he lavished upon us.
> (Eph. 1:5-6; 2:8; 1:7-8)

Most of the time, we in the church reverse the process of forgiveness. We ask people to repent before we extend forgiveness. We demand moral change before granting pardon. But:

> God's forgiveness is logically and psychologically *before* rather than, as usually conceived, *after* repentance. Honest confession is not a condition for pardon. It is rather, our way of becoming seriously aware of the pardon which is already there. Pardon announces what only honest confession is able to hear.[22]

These truths light the spark for spiritual renewal in the church. If somebody has to "shape up" before they come to a therapy or counseling group, all is lost. If they come to a household of "righteous" people, they will be defensive and healing will not take place. But if atonement has been offered and pardon already extended, then the context for confession or repentance is made available. It is worth noting that Jesus came preaching that "the Kingdom of God is at hand, repent" (Mark 1:15). He did not put it the other way that one must "repent, and the Kingdom of God will come." If the church can become "one beggar telling another beggar where to find bread," then there is real hope for a revitalized evangelism.

Perhaps more than any other modern theologian, Paul Tillich clarified grace for modern men with his word "acceptance." I recall vividly some years ago giving Tillich's sermon on acceptance to a young woman who was in a psychiatric ward. She was a member of the church, but she always came late to services. Her hair was in perfect array; her clothing was immaculate. In fact, she looked like a painted china doll. She was in the hospital because of emotional breakdown. She was trying desperately to put up a front of perfection. Her psychiatrist was trying to help her achieve self-acceptance; I was trying to help her understand that she was accepted by God. One day, after an hour's interview with her doctor, she stepped into the chapel in the Catholic hospital and knelt down to pray.

Suddenly it dawned within her. God accepted her just as she was, and she could accept herself. When she returned to her ward other young women patients could tell by the radiance on her face that something had happened to her. When I saw her, she had washed the excessive make-up from her face, had combed her hair, and was sitting relaxed. Within a few days she was released from the hospital.

Tillich writes,

> It is not an exaggeration to say that today man experiences his present situation in terms of disruption, conflict, self-destruction, meaninglessness, and despair in all realms of life. . . . The question arising out of this experience is not, as in the Reformation, the question of a merciful God and the forgiveness of sins; nor is it, as in the early Greek church, the question of finitude, of death, and error, nor is it the question of the personal religious life or of the Christianization of culture and society. It is the question of a reality in which the self-estrangement of our existence is overcome, a reality of reconciliation and reunion, of creativity, meaning, and hope.[23]

The reason that Tillich is so profound is that he understands that mere forgiveness of a moral failure is not all we need. We need acceptance of our very being. Our anxiety cannot be relieved except in accepting relationships. If the church is to have an evangelism today, we must be ready to look at the question of estrangement and salvation in something more than "moral" terms. Man's condition is estrangement or separation. Salvation is reconciliation, healing, the bestowal of wholeness. Moralistic concepts of guilt and forgiveness are valid, but they are not big enough categories to contain the whole of grace. A legalistic calculation of praise and blame blocks rather than bolsters healing. Acceptance, as it is experienced in a counseling group (or in *koinonia*) transcends forgiveness. It bespeaks of the healing power of God, overcoming our basic anxieties and our separation from him. People in *koinonia* still doubt, still make mistakes, still struggle with problems of communication, but they gradually become aware that they are not alone. They slowly perceive that the group is standing with them and that somehow God loves them with no strings attached. In the great sermon "You are Accepted" Tillich describes the experience in which "grace strikes us." [24] These include experiences of guilt, but also include those times when "we walk through the dark valley of a dark and meaningless and empty life." And he insists that no particular form or mode of the experience of acceptance can be prescribed. "Nothing is demanded of this experience, no religious, or moral, or intellectual presupposition."

> You are accepted, accepted by that which is greater than you, and the name of which you do not know. Do not ask for the name now; perhaps you will find it later. Do not try to do anything now; perhaps later you will do much. Do not seek for anything; do not perform anything; do not intend anything. Simply accept the fact that you are accepted. [25]

Moralists will be quick to jump on these words and demand to know where is the moral transformation, just as across the centuries the church has continually twisted Paul's doctrine of grace. There is a time for growth, and it will come as surely as a flower will bloom with sunshine and rain. Luther said that you do not have to tell a stone lying in the sun to be warm. Paul does have a "therefore" in his theology which places severe moral imperatives on the community, but it occurs as an admonition to the children of

God. Couples in marriage groups began to build budgets, stop their wild drunken orgies, pray for peace in the world, tithe to the church, wash communion glasses at midnight on Christmas Eve, urge other troubled couples to seek help, etc., but none of these things were demanded of them. They were the fruits of healthy hearts. Tillich in another sermon writes that "people are sick not only because they have not received love, but because they are not allowed to give it." [26]

This theological excursion may seem irrelevant to some seeking a gimmick for evangelism or wanting a quick answer to the need for spiritual outreach. But it is the hinge on which the doors turns. If we understand grace, we can form *koinonia* groups and not be afraid if barefoot, long haired young adults attend. If we comprehend a community of acceptance, there is no marriage, no matter how "morally rotten" but which can move toward healing and discovering the love of God.

To be quite specific, I am convinced that there are two distinct evangelistic thrusts which spring from this understanding of grace and community. *First,* there is the opportunity for treatment/growth groups. These groups are necessarily professional, led by skilled pastors and highly trained laymen. They are composed of people in grave distress. But second, there are opportunities for many types of sharing groups which practice the experience of *koinonia.* Men everywhere, in their heart of hearts, are hungry for honest relationships of mutual concern. In his article on "Evangelism Through Small Groups" Dr. Roger Birkman, Director of "Discovery Groups" in Houston, Texas, tells of his use of psychological testing procedures coupled with the kind of sharing we have been discussing to bring about

151

Christian fellowship and spiritual growth with normal individuals. He writes,

> The value of such groups in the evangelistic program of the church is basically two-fold; it is an immediate means of bringing new members into a warm fellowship, and it is an effective means for reclaiming members who are neither using their talents nor making contributions to the Church.[27]

Social Action

This whole approach to ministry could be criticized as being so personalistic that it avoids the great social issues of our time—war, famine, racial bigotry, pollution, and poverty. However, it is obvious that some social problems have their beginnings in homes where there is a sick marriage. A home where healing is happening is preventive medicine against many social ills.

There is even more to be said. Something happens to people who have been working together for emotional and spiritual growth. In their sensitivity to the needs of others, they are more sensitive to societal injustices that stifle personal development. In recent community efforts to start a drug council and helping house, a number of our couples were eager to give assistance. One woman who is now quite active in a peace movement wrote in her evaluation, "Now that I know that God loves every single person in the world, I know that peace and love are His will for all mankind." From their own experience of acceptance, they are slow to reject kids with long hair, in contrast to the "up tight" people who are thinking in categorical rather than human terms.

One thing is certain, *Out of the marriage counseling*

groups came a great concern for marriages and family life in our society. Pastor and people became much more interested in marriage and divorce laws, mental health facilities, counseling and family service centers, practices of the juvenile authorities, interest rates for installment buying, and legal aspects of birth control and abortion. Their concern for one another gradually developed a growing concern for the welfare of other people.

The Pastor Himself

Deep within each pastor is the desire to help lead people into a closer relationship to God. He prays for that kind of fellowship within the church which is an actual participation in the spirit of Christ and in the lives of one another. He yearns for that kind of power within himself and within the community of faithful that permits emotional, physical, and spiritual healings to take place. The minister of God reads with a certain nostalgia words like these,

> So those who received his word were baptized, and there were added that day about three thousand souls. And they devoted themselves to the apostles' teaching and fellowship [koinonia], to the breaking of bread and the prayers (Acts 2:41).

As one called by Jesus to be a physician of souls, he longs to have in his company men and women who have "been healed of evil spirits and infirmities" (Luke 8:2).

In my participation in marriage counseling groups my hope was restored in the present workings of God's Spirit. The ministry became exciting to me once again as I saw the lives of people change before my eyes. While I cannot report the world changing its course of orbit or a Wesleyan revival, it is nevertheless a source of inestimable joy to me to realize that over twenty-five homes are radically different because of our mutual involvement. My own marriage is more flexible, more open, more communicative because Julia and I participated in the marriage explorations of others.

The Holy Communion has become more meaningful for me, just as it has for some of our couples. In the Lord's Supper, it is not the individual believer who receives from the Lord, but the fellowship of believers who receive also from each other. The Lord's Supper has taken on for me the shape of a family meal. Now, for me, whenever a man partakes of the bread and wine, he is pronounced OK.

Living room churches no longer seem threatening to me as a professional clergyman. Now I pray for them, encourage them, and try to keep in touch with them, even if they are not counted in the statistical ecclesiastical reports. I am not upset if there are more conversions there than occur under my preaching. Through our group work I feel a certain kinship with the New Testament churches and with the Wesleyan societies.

Professionally I can hold up my head. We have been able to heal, as pastors, illnesses that physicians could not cure. We have been able to reconcile couples who could not be helped by attorneys. We have been able to provide ongoing insight and support which would not be provided by psychiatric hospitals or psychiatrists. I have felt involved in life at its deepest dimension. When I began the group counseling procedure, my hopes were to reconcile marriages, much as would a marriage counselor or psychologist. I quickly saw that there were spiritual dimensions beyond my dreams. The needs came right from the soul; reconciliation came right from the heart of God. These words, written by a man who had been a part of a life changing group experience, point to the mystery of the *koinonia* encounter.

> We laughed—but it was more than laughter—it was some new kind of joy—from sharing together a long while. It almost seemed (don't smile) a prayer of some kind to be here with each other in a moment like this. (We knew too that this moment had such fullness only because of what we brought to it—the painful and the pleasant, the curious and the known, the secret and the public, the words and the silences, the you and the me.)
> And together now, (in this laughter-moment) we take part in something else—community.[28]

My wife and I and over a score of couples feel that we have some knowledge of what St. Paul was feeling when he wrote: "So if there is any encouragement in Christ, any incentive of love, any participation in the Spirit, any affection and sympathy, complete my joy by being of the same mind" (Phil. 2:1-3). "The grace of the Lord Jesus Christ and the love of God and the fellowship of the Holy Spirit be with you all" (II Cor. 13:14).

Appendix A

Individual Evaluation Questionnaire for Marriage Counseling Groups

1. Why did you first come to the marriage counseling group? Were you hesitant to come? Why?

2. As you remember the dynamics of the group this year, what was happening within the group during the sessions?

3. What did the leader do?

4. Were there any times when you wanted to drop out? What kept you from it?

5. Was meeting in the pastor's home helpful or harmful? Why?

6. List several people or couples (other than yourself and your spouse) whom you believe were helped. What happened to them?

7. Who was not helped? Why?

8. What happened to your spouse?

9. What happened to you?

10. Has the year been helpful? Why?

11. Would you rather be emotionally, spiritually, and maritally where you were a year ago or where you are now?

12. How has the marriage counseling group affected your relationship to God? To the Church?

13. What do you see to be your needs in the future? Your marriage needs? The needs of the group?

14. What has been the most significant spiritual experience of your life? What has been the most significant spiritual experience of the past year?

15. In your marriage, what changes have taken place in the following areas:

   (a) financial

   (b) relationships to children

   (c) sexual

   (d) family—inlaws, etc.

   (e) communications

   (f) quantity and quality of time spent together as a couple

Appendix B

Case History
John and Marie Rutherford
1971

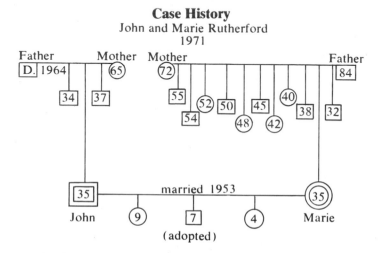

Intake and Initial Interviews

Mrs. Rutherford (Marie) called on the telephone, asking to see me. We set an appointment for the following day. She came by herself and arrived a few minutes early. Since she is an attractive woman who keeps an immaculate home, I was a bit surprised to note her very informal, almost sloppy clothing and half-combed hair.

Reason for Coming

Marie indicated that she and her husband John had been married seventeen years and that she "just couldn't take it anymore." She expressed a deep hunger for affection and said that he was unwilling to provide any.

Marie made no threats—perhaps one half-hearted hint of divorce.

As her pastor, I had been in their home on a couple of

158

John was very concerned.

The next week, they arrived on time. She had quit her diet pills. I talked about the group; they were ready to participate. They promised to contact the Reverend Marshall Stanton, group counselor, immediately, and they did so. (I had promised him that I would assist him in forming his first group.)

Here is his evaluation of their entrance into the group after three weeks of experience.

Evaluation by Stanton

Marie was a tense person who expressed herself strongly. She began criticizing the cub scout program. He seemed slightly annoyed about her talking about this in our first encounter. When the group arrived that evening they were quite pleasant.

The Rutherfords came in separately for the tests on Sunday afternoon (M.M.P.I. tests with Yokefellow insight slips).

Our most recent session is the best in terms of interaction. We began talking about the four demons which plague the emotional life, Fear, Guilt, Inferiority Feelings, and Misguided Love (hatred). As we got to John, he paused quite a while and then said, "I think I am pretty normal in all those areas, but there must be something wrong in some of them or I wouldn't have all the problems I have."

Marie looked at the list and said, "Gee, I don't know. I think all of those are on the top." She talked about how it was to be raised an Italian who was looked down upon, at least while she was growing up.

Much of this evening John's nonverbals were to withdraw. He sat in his chair with his legs crossed. He doesn't smile or look hostile. He just sits and observes. His only comment was one which he just volunteered. He said that he didn't think he knew for sure what love was.

The pattern seems to be coming through that John doesn't comprehend emotion. He doesn't know how to cope with strong emotions. Marie is full of emotion. I get the feeling that John tries to operate very rationally most of the time, and his wife operates very emotionally most of the time.

A Halfway Evaluation

I observed that John is beginning to come alive. He identifies

occasions, and I knew that their three children were adopted. I asked if there were reasons why she had not been able to have natural birth children. The doctors felt that they should be able to have children of their own. I asked how their sexual relationship had been, and she indicated that they had sexual relations only once every few months practically ever since they were married.

I thought I could help them and asked if Mr. Rutherford would be willing to come in. She said she didn't know, but that she would ask him.

Intake and Initial Interviews

Personal interview with John

He was pleasant, willing to become involved, though he expressed some doubt that she would stay with any significant program. He was quiet He looked directly at me, did not fidget or smoke or look around He takes pride in being a good provider, a successful businessman.

At night, he says he likes to watch TV, but that Marie wants to talk. He likes to go out with her to sporting events; she wants to stay home with the children and doesn't like sports. He says she should be interested in things going on in the world (like on TV), but she won't sit down and watch with him. He admits that he is not very affectionate, either verbally or in physical expressions.

He says she is very dogmatic and opinionated "just like an Italian" and that the weight problem is probably normal because of her Italian background and build.

Description of Clients

Both Mr. and Mrs. Rutherford are thirty-five years of age. They grew up together. They went to the same high school and married shortly after graduation. He was from a family of English descent, a family that owned their business. He was Protestant, sent to Sunday school and youth meetings, but his family usually worked on Sunday.

Marie's family is Italian Catholic. Her father was from the old country and was very strict, even harsh, with his children, particularly his daughters. Marie felt very little warmth from her parents.

Marie is olive skinned, with dark brunette hair, not too tall, and at the present time, quite overweight.

In the office she is open and expressive, even volatile, forceful, with strong views and opinions. She sits relaxed and totally involved. She looks at John hoping to get some word or expression from him.

John is of medium height, blond crew cut, somewhat stocky build, with a slight paunch. He thinks a long time before he speaks. He usually comes directly from his business, often arriving a few minutes late.

John does not express much hostility. He does not interrupt Marie. He looks at me rather than at her and speaks to me about her rather than to her.

Background Information (additional)

Both John and Marie indicate a lack of warmth in their relationships with their parents.

During the first fourteen years of their marriage, they both worked hard together—getting their own business established. They both worked twelve to fourteen hours a day, seven days a week. During the past three years, however, as the business has become so successful, Marie has not worked, but has stayed home with the children. During these three years her weight problem has become increasingly severe.

They have few friends. They don't go places very much.

First conjoint interview (following two more individual sessions —one with each)

I couldn't believe how quiet they both were when they sat down. I decided to experiment with a technique I'd been reading about called "Interpersonal Perception Method" (Laing, Phillipson, and Lee).

I gave each of them a pad and pencil and asked them to write three or four sentences on the following four questions.

a) What is my view of myself?
b) What is my view of my mate?
c) What does my mate think about me?
d) What does my mate think I think of him/her?

Here is a verbatim of their write-ups:

Mrs. R.: a) I am bad tempered—dull—feel deep a lot of things but not able to get these across in the right way.

b) He's generous beyond belief with things. He's very smart, knows s about most everything, only failure i ability to show loving feelings for us.

c) I don't have the slightest idea what about me.

d) I think he thinks I expect too much that I'm unreasonable and that he's best. Ha! Emotionally that is.

Whereas she wrote quickly in pencil, with da flourish, he wrote slowly, carefully, crossing out an word, sometimes starting again.

Mr. R.: a) I am a good provider, a fairly goo man, I am not overly affectionate. might be undersexed.

b) She is a very good mother. She is a housewife. She is somewhat domin has a strong will. She is easily dep needs love and affection to live happ

c) She thinks I am a fairly good pro doesn't think I am a very good lover

d) She thinks that I think she is over unattractive, but this changes cons she is in good spirits or depressed.

As we went along, alternating readings and comm apparent to me that I had arranged a pretty highly interview, yet real feelings, though carefully soften to be coming out.

Introduction to Group Counseling

In a later interview I mentioned our use of mar counseling. They expressed some hesitancy. Mari fears of sharing with other people.

During January, they had a crisis. John showe Marie was so upset she did not come. She had star pills that week, and they were making her nervous.

things get started—maybe somewhere along the line you try to talk about some things and you don't get anywhere, so you just quit trying. I need to be able to recognize the way people feel."

Conclusion: After Six Months of Group Counseling

John has opened up more and more. He has been willing to express some of his feelings. Whenever he talks, Marie listens closely. He does not always wait until he has carefully thought through a sentence before he states it. He sits without crossing his legs or folding his arms. He looks at Marie sometimes when he says what he feels.

Marie became aware that part of her loquaciousness was anxiety. Talking was often a cover-up for her feelings of insecurity. She had interpreted John's silence as great "Olympian" strength. When he began to express feelings of anxiety or unsureness, she was surprised.

John was surprised when nobody clobbered him for having feelings. He was pleased when Marie felt good about his modest expressions of love.

In the group, it became apparent to both John and Marie that they held one great common experience—their compulsive need to work. It was hard work which had brought them together. As long as they had been working side by side, things hadn't been too bad. They decided to sell their business and go to another city and build a new business together from the ground up.

Before they left town, I saw them one night, sitting alone together like a young couple in love, drinking coffee in a dimly lit restaurant. They were talking softly as if they were the only persons in the world. In addition, they presented gifts to both the Reverend Stanton and myself and indicated that John was expressing himself to her, and she was listening carefully to the expressions of affection when they came. The weight problem wasn't solved, but it didn't seem to be bothering them so much.

Appendix C

Outline for Intake Interview

(Form for recording first interview summary)

I. Face Sheet Information: The necessary information for the face sheet may be acquired in the beginning of the interview or at the end, whichever seems more appropriate.

II. Referal: How did the client know about you? How does he feel about having been referred to you, and how does he understand the reason for being referred? Even if he was self-referred it still may be important to know how he happened to come to you.

III. Reaction to Coming: How does the client feel about coming to you for counseling? He may have to be helped to express feelings of reluctance in coming to you. Is he able to admit his anxiety or does he have to deny it? Success in dealing with this initial feeling often determines the direction of the interview.

IV. Presenting Problem: What does the client see as his major problem: Does he see it as a marital problem or an internal problem? How long has it been a problem? Was there a precipitating event which brought the problem to a head? How do significant others in his life see the problem, and how have they tried to deal with it before he came for help?

V. Help Desired: What solution, if any, does the client see as desirable, and how does he expect the counseling to be of help to him? How have you as counselor interpreted to him your ability to help?

VI. Help Offered: What kind of agreement did you make with the client? How did the two of you interpret what you would be able to do and was there mutual agreement about this?

VII. Counselor's Impression of the Client: What are the counselor's impressions of the client? What are the real problems he brings? If a marital problem, what is the nature of the marital conflict? Is this client suitable for counseling, or is there a need for referral? In addition to these relatively objective impressions, how does the counselor feel about the client personally? Estimate the influence, if any, this feeling may have upon the subsequent process.

VIII. Interaction in Marital Situations: If husband and wife are seen together at this or a second interview, how do the difficulties involved in the marriage show themselves in the interaction of husband and wife?

IX. Disposition: What issues or problems are apparent to the counselor regarding the assignment of the client (couple) for counseling or referral? What plans, if any, were made in regard to appointment times or other arrangements necessary?

Note: It is certainly not necessary during an interview to plow through this outline in a straight blind furrow. An openended interview will produce for you most of the information required; you should engage in a brief review of the outline before the interview closes to make sure all information is available. If you are a slave of the outline during the interview you may get accurate information but will "pay for it" by losing genuine contact with the client.

Notes

I

1. Editorial, *The Salina Journal,* March 17, 1971.
2. In 1971, on the basis of our early experiences, I wrote a booklet for the Family Enrichment Bureau and Tidings entitled "The Pastor and Marriage Therapy Groups." Even though my own definitions were clear, it caused some confusion in professional circles. Group counseling is a more generally accepted term.
3. William R. Parker and Elaine St. Johns, *Prayer Can Change Your Life* (Englewood Cliffs, N. J.: Prentice-Hall, 1957).
4. Jeanette G. Targow and Robert V. Zweber, "Participants' Reactions to Treatment in a Married Couples' Group," *International Journal of Group Psychotherapy,* 19 (1969), 221.

II

1. Neal Daniels, "Participation of Relatives in a Group Centered Program," *International Journal of Group Psychotherapy,* 17 (1967), 336.
2. William E. Hulme, *Pastoral Care Come of Age* (Nashville: Abingdon Press, 1970), p. 15.
3. George R. Bach and Peter Wyden, *The Intimate Enemy* (New York: Avon Books, 1968), pp. 50-51.
4. Joseph W. Knowles, *Group Counseling* (Philadelphia: Fortress Press, 1964), p. 15.
5. C. L. Bruninga, "Group Marriage Counseling in a State Hospital," *Hospital and Community Psychiatry,* 18 (Dec., 1967), 379.
6. Phillip A. Anderson, "A Ministry To Troubled People," *Pastoral Psychology,* 19 (Sept., 1968), 20.

III

1. Joseph Havens, "Christs to One Another," *The New Shape of Pastoral Theology,* ed. William B. Oglesby, Jr. (New York: Abingdon Press, 1969), p. 251.

2. Dorothy Semenow Garwood, "The Significance and Dynamics of Sensitivity Training Programs," *International Journal of Group Psychotherapy,* XVII (Oct., 1967), 458.

3. *Ibid.,* p. 457.

4. Maurice E. Linden and Hilda M. Goodwin and Harvey Resnik, "Group Psychotherapy of Couples in Marriage Counseling," *International Journal of Group Psychotherapy,* 18 (1968), 313.

5. Knowles, *Group Counseling,* pp. 67-72.

6. George R. Bach, *Intensive Group Psychotherapy* (New York: The Ronald Press, 1954), p. 17.

7. Knowles, *Group Counseling,* p. 23.

8. Paul W. Pruyser, "The Use and Neglect of Pastoral Resources," *Pastoral Psychology* 23 (Sept., 1972), 5-17.

IV

1. Victor Bloom and Shirley I. Dobie, "The Effect of Observers on the Process of Group Therapy," *International Journal of Group Psychotherapy,* XIX (Jan. 1969), 79-86.

2. Fern J. Azima, "Interaction and Insight in Group Psychotherapy: the Case for Insight," *International Journal of Group Psychotherapy,* XIX (July, 1969), 261.

3. Hulme, *Pastoral Care Come of Age,* p. 17.

4. Irving Harris, "Finding a Handle," *Groups That Work* (Grand Rapids, Mich.: Zondervan Publishing House, 1967), p. 13.

5. Knowles, *Group Counseling,* p. 15.

6. *Ibid.,* p. 16.

7. Paul Tournier, *The Person Reborn* (New York: Harper & Row, 1966), p. 118.

8. Theodore O. Wedel, "Interpersonal Groups and the Church," *The Creative Role of Interpersonal Groups in the Church Today,* ed. John L. Casteel (New York: Association Press, 1968), pp. 42-48.

9. Howard J. Clinebell, Jr., "Enriching Marriages in the 70's", (Pittsburg, Pa: Thesis Theological Cassettes), vol. 3, no. 5, side 1.

10. Reuel Howe, *The Miracle of Dialogue* (New York: The Seabury Press, 1963), p. 23.

11. T. S. Eliot, "The Cocktail Party," *The Complete Poems and*

Plays (New York: Harcourt, Brace & Co., 1952), p. 342.

12. Robert A. Edgar, "Listening to Others," *The Creative Role of Interpersonal Groups in the Church Today,* ed. John L. Casteel, p. 173.

13. Ibid., p. 179.

14. Ibid., p. 182.

15. Howe, *The Miracle of Dialogue,* p. 3.

16. Paul W. Pruyser, "The Master Hand: Psychological Notes on Pastoral Blessing," *The New Shape of Pastoral Theology,* p. 363.

17. Karl Menninger, *Love Against Hate* (New York: Harcourt, Brace & World, 1942), p. 260.

18. Mowrer, *The New Group Therapy* (Princeton, N.J.: D. Van Nostrand Co., 1964), p. 27.

V

1. Hulme, *Pastoral Care Come of Age,* p. 46.

2. Seward Hiltner, *The Counselor in Counseling* (New York: Abingdon-Cokesbury Press, 1950), p. 148.

3. Howe, *The Miracle of Dialogue,* p. 73.

4. Knowles, *Group Counseling,* p. 42.

5. Howe, *The Miracle of Dialogue,* p. 71.

6. Knowles, *Group Counseling,* pp. 45-50.

7. Linden, Goodwin, and Resnick, "Group Psychotherapy of Couples in Marriage Counseling," p. 317.

8. Richard N. Robertson, Leonard T. Maholick, and David Shapiro, "The Parish Minister as Counselor: A Dilemma and Challenge," *Pastoral Psychology* (June, 1969), 26.

9. Charles Wheeler Scott, "The Cure of Souls," *Pastoral Psychology,* 20 (Mar., 1969), 5.

10. Joseph W. Knowles, "The Counseling Group," *The Creative Role of Interpersonal Groups in the Church Today,* p. 132.

11. Seward Hiltner, *Ferment in The Ministry* (Nashville: Abingdon Press, 1970).

12. Jacques Duquesne, *A Church Without Priests* (Toronto: Macmillan, 1969), p. 90.

13. Knowles, *Group Counseling,* p. 26.

14. *Ibid.,* p. 30.

15. Charles H. Dickinson, "Marriage Counselor Laws: Are They Adequate?" *Handbook of Marriage Counseling,* p. 407.

16. Richard B. Wilke, "The Pastor and Marriage Therapy Groups" (Escanaba, Mich.: Upper Pennisula Family Life Bureau, 1971).

17. Richard B. Wilke, *Tell Me Again, I'm Listening* (Nashville: Abingdon Press, 1973).

VI

1. Robert A. Raines, *Reshaping the Christian Life* (New York: Harper & Row, 1964), p. 10.
2. *Ibid.,* p. 11.
3. *Ibid.,* p. 23.
4. *Ibid.,* p. 17.
5. J. Y. Campbell, *Three New Testament Studies* (Leiden, Germany: E. J. Brill, 1965), republished and presented to him by his friends with an appreciation, pp. 1-2.
6. Blaine B. Rader, "Koinonia and the Therapeutic Relationship," *Pastoral Psychology* 21 (Oct., 1970), 40.
7. Robert Spike, *Tests of a Living Church* (New York: Association Press, 1961), p. 20.
8. Bruce Larson, "Honesty is the Only Policy," *Groups That Work,* p. 20.
9. George William Bowman III, *The Dynamics of Confession* (Richmond, Va.: John Knox Press, 1969), p. 17.
10. *Ibid.,* p. 17.
11. *Ibid.,* p. 32.
12. Mowrer, *The New Group Therapy,* pp. 18-19.
13. Carl Jung, *Modern Man in Search of a Soul* (New York: Harcourt, Brace and World, 1933), p. 34.
14. Oscar Wilde, quoted by Bowman, *The Dynamics of Confession,* p. 30.
15. Walter Nigg, *Warriors of God* (New York: Alfred A. Knopf, 1959), p. 76.
16. Taizé Community, *The Rule of Taizé* (Taizé, France: Les Presses de Taizé, 1965).
17. Eberhard Bethge, *Dietrich Bonhoeffer* (New York: Harper & Row, 1970), p. 384.
18. Mary A. Thomson, "O Zion Haste," *The Methodist Hymnal* (Nashville: The Methodist Publishing House, 1969), No. 299.
19. Dag Hammarskjold, *Markings* (New York: Alfred A. Knopf, 1965), p. 38.
20. Tracey K. Jones, Jr., *Our Mission Today* (New York: World Outlook Press, 1963), p. 110.
21. Thomas C. Oden, "The Priority of Pardon to Penitence," *Pastoral Psychology,* 20 (Apr., 1969) 19-20.
22. *Ibid.,* p. 19.

23. Daniel Day Williams, "Paul Tillich's Doctrine of Forgiveness," *Pastoral Psychology,* 19 (Feb., 1968), 18.

24. Tillich, "You Are Accepted," *The Shaking of the Foundations* (New York: Charles Scribner's Sons, 1948), p. 162.

25. *Ibid.,* p. 162.

26. Paul Tillich, *The New Being* (New York: Charles Scribner's Sons, 1955), p. 48.

27. Roger W. Birkman, "Evangelism Through Small Groups," *Pastoral Psychology,* 19 (June, 1968), p. 43.

28. "Intimacy," Human Development Institute, Atlanta, Ga., a division of Bell and Howell, (Cassettes and workbooks)

Bibliography

Theological and Psychological Background

Berne, Eric. *Games People Play*. New York: Grove Press, 1964.

Bowman, George William, III. *The Dynamics of Confession*. Richmond, Virginia: John Knox Press, 1969.

Campbell, J. Y. *Three New Testament Studies*. Leiden. E. J. Brill, 1965. Republished and presented to him by his friends with an appreciation.

Groskreutz, Donald A. "A Person Centered Theology," *The New Shape of Pastoral Theology*, ed. by William B. Oglesby, Jr. Nashville: Abingdon Press, 1969.

Harris, Thomas H. *I'm O K, You're O K*. New York: Harper & Row, 1967.

Howe, Reuel L. *The Miracle of Dialogue*. New York: The Seabury Press, 1963.

Menninger, Karl. *Love Against Hate*. New York: Harcourt, Brace & World, 1942.

Osborne, Cecil G. *The Art of Understanding Yourself*. Grand Rapids, Michigan: Zondervan Publishing House, 1967.

Pruyser, Paul W. "The Master Hand: Psychological Notes on Pastoral Blessing." *The New Shape of Pastoral Theology*, ed. by William S. Oglesby, Jr.

————. "The Use and Neglect of Pastoral Resources," *Pastoral Psychology*, 23 (Sept., 1972) 5-17.

Taizé Community. *The Rule of Taizé*. In French and in English, Les Presses de Taizé, 1965.

Tournier, Paul. *The Person Reborn*, trans. by Edwin Hudson. New York: Harper & Row, 1966.

Watzlawick, Paul; Beavin, Janet Helmick; and Jackson, Don D. *Pragmatics of Human Communications.* New York: W. W. Norton & Company, 1967.

Group Work and Group Therapy

Anderson, Philip A. "A Ministry to Troubled People," *Pastoral Psychology,* 19 (Sept., 1968), 20-26.

Anthony, E. James. "Reflections on Twenty-five Years of Group Psychotherapy," *International Journal of Group Psychotherapy,* 18 (1968), 312-15.

Bach, George R. *Intensive Group Psychotherapy.* New York: The Ronald Press, 1954.

Bach, George R., and Wyden, Peter. *The Intimate Enemy.* New York: Avon Books, 1968.

Bruninga, C. L. "Group Marriage Counseling in a State Hospital," *Hospital and Community Psychiatry,* 18 (Dec., 1967), 379-82.

Casteel, John L., ed. *The Creative Role of Interpersonal Groups in the Church Today.* New York: Association Press, 1968.

Corsini, Raymond J. *Methods of Group Psychotherapy.* New York: McGraw-Hill Book Co., 1957.

Havens, Joseph. "Christs to One Another," *The New Shape of Pastoral Theology,* ed. by William B. Oglesby, Jr.

Knowles, Joseph W. *Group Counseling.* Englewood Cliffs, N. J. Prentice-Hall, 1964.

Mowrer, O. Hobart. *The New Group Therapy.* Princeton, N. J.: D. Van Nostrand Co., 1964.

Reid, Clyde. *Groups Alive—Church Alive.* New York: Harper & Row, 1969.

Rogers, Carl, *Carl Rogers on Encounter Groups.* New York: Harper & Row, 1971.

Scott, Charles Wheeler. "The Cure of Souls," *Pastoral Psychology.* 20 (Mar., 1969), 5-7.

Yokefellows, Inc. *New Dimensions in Spiritual Growth.* A booklet printed by Yokefellows, Inc., 209 Park Road, Burlingame, Calif.

Pastoral Counseling

Ard, Ben N. and Constance C. *Handbook of Marriage Counseling*. Palo Alto, Calif.: Science and Behavior Books, 1969.

Dicks, Russell L. *Pastoral Work and Personal Counseling*. New York: The Macmillan Co., 1964.

Elliott, Robert E. "Motherly and Fatherly Modes of Pastoral Care," *The New Shape of Pastoral Theology*, ed. by William B. Oglesby, Jr.

Hiltner, Seward. *Ferment in the Ministry*. Nashville: Abingdon Press, 1969.

Robertson, Richard N.; Maholick, Leonard T.; and Shapiro, David. "The Parish Minister as Counselor: A Dilemma and Challenge," *Pastoral Psychology*, (June, 1969), 24-29.

Stewart, Charles William. *The Minister As Marriage Counselor*. Nashville: Abingdon Press, 1961.

Marriage

Clinebell, Howard J. and Charlotte H. *The Intimate Marriage*. New York: Harper & Row, 1970.

Mace, David R. *The Christian Response to the Sexual Revolution*. Nashville: Abingdon Press, 1970.

————. *Getting Ready for Marriage*. Nashville: Abingdon Press, 1972.

————. *We Can Have Better Marriages*. Nashville: Abingdon Press, 1974.

Shedd, Charlie W. *Letters to Karen*. Nashville: Abingdon Press, 1965.

————. *Letters to Philip*. Garden City, N. J.: Doubleday, 1968.

Steinmetz, Urban G. "Marriage Enrichment Program." Escanaba, Michigan: Upper Pennisula Family Life Bureau, 1965. (Lecture Series on 33⅓ records)

Tournier, Paul. *To Understand Each Other*, trans. by John S. Gilmour. Richmond, Va.: John Knox Press, 1967.

Wilke, Richard B. *Tell Me Again, I'm Listening*. Nashville: Abingdon Press, 1973.